FOREWORD BY MIRIAM GONZÁLEZ DURÁNTEZ

7 TRAITS
OF
HIGHLY SUCCESSFUL
WOMEN
ON BOARDS

VIEWS FROM THE TOP AND
HOW TO GET THERE

DR. YVONNE THOMPSON CBE

7 TRAITS OF HIGHLY SUCCESSFUL WOMEN ON BOARDS

VIEWS FROM THE TOP AND HOW TO GET THERE

First published in 2014 by

Panoma Press Ltd
48 St Vincent Drive, St Albans, Herts, AL1 5SJ, UK
info@panomapress.com
www.panomapress.com

Book layout by Michael Inns
Artwork by Karen Gladwell

ISBN 978-1-909623-73-6

Contents

"I read Yvonne's book with a highlighter in hand - lots of great advice and words of wisdom that I want to revisit. In order to encourage and inspire more women to set their sights on corporate boards, we need to increase the profile of and access to those women who are already there. This book does just that, bringing their stories and experiences to life. We are making progress, but we can't afford to lose momentum. We have to keep this discussion very much in the mainstream."

Brenda Trenowden, *Chair 30% Club and Managing Director, ANZ*

"The 7 Traits of Highly Successful Women On Boards is a must read for women and men in the workplace. It highlights the real life challenges that face women in the workplace AND most importantly how they have overcome them. What I love most about this book is that it makes the boardroom accessible, it is inclusive and provides real models rather than role models. I believe that this book will stimulate a significant increase in the number of women who aspire to have a seat in the boardroom and the number of men who welcome them. Thompson's lessons from the boardroom are refreshingly authentic and unapologetic, a perfect antidote to the fix of women's literature."

Jenny Garrett, *Award Winning Coach and Author of Rocking Your Role*

"This book can inspire more women to come back into their careers with enthusiasm, and in turn can gravitate to the board room, or young women to continue with their careers. I hope it will inspire them to go for it because the need is there and the demand is there. We need approximately 250 more women into those board rooms to reach the 25% target over the next couple of years. I'd like to congratulate you on writing this book the timing is excellent and I think it will be an inspiration."

Sir John Parker, *Chairman Anglo American*

TESTIMONIALS

"Yvonne Thompson tackles an important and topical issue, in an original and thoughtful way. The women she has interviewed are from a diverse mix of backgrounds, experience and skills. Yet, they have all beaten the odds in getting to where they sit today. The author has teased out synergies and differences to present a compelling read. Society – and business – cannot afford to sit back and wait for more women to gain board experience. We need to be proactive in this area. This book plays a part in highlighting the issue and offering insight into possible solutions."

Professor Alison Wride, *Provost, GSM London*

"I have to admit that I am not a fan of biographies. However, this book has defied my prejudice. There is something in this book for everyone. The book combines biographical story-telling, personal insights and honest advice-provision. Yvonne has enabled individual personalities and personal philosophies to shine through whilst also pulling together common themes and packaging up useful lessons in a neat format. The very diverse range of experiences and insights from 22 highly talented women have been presented in an engaging and enlightening format, so that any would be female careerist can learn something from this book and apply it to her own success whether she is aiming for the boardroom or not. The positive energy demonstrated by these leaders, through thick and thin, is the residing take-away message for me. A positive mind-set has fuelled these women's adaptation to changing circumstances and sustained their personal and professional growth. They all demonstrate a very down-to-earth attitude about their success and their mindfulness of their impact on those around them is the hallmark of an authentic leader. An interesting read for any woman wanting to learn from real life experience."

Rachel Short, *Director YSC London*

"In my experience of running women's leadership programs women love to listen to other women's stories of how they reached the top. They are always deeply personal, moving and inspiring experiences. If we want more women on boards, which we certainly do, then we must showcase the positive experiences women have on boards and the routes they took to get there. Yvonne Thompson has achieved both of these tasks very successfully with her book."

Professor Susan Vinnicombe CBE, *Cranfield University School of Management*

T E S T I M O N I A L S

ACKNOWLEDGMENTS

WITHOUT DOING an Academy Award Best Actress acceptance speech, there are some people in the foreground and background of my life who have provided me with the nourishment, encouragement and wisdom without which this book would not have not been possible.

First among them is a man I met over 20 years ago. Of course I did not know it at the time but this man would be like a North Star in my professional life. He understood that I was a frustrated writer, and in a conversation during one of our bi-annual lunches he, understanding my obstruction, influenced me to write a book about an area that I have spent my whole professional life championing: women, equality, and diversity. He is Hugh Harris CBE of London First. During our last lunch, at the Commonwealth Club, Hugh asked me how the book was coming along. At this point my efforts were conceptual and very much a theoretical construct existing purely in my head. He then made an intervention that would give me the much needed impetus to kick start the writing of this book. Being a networker extraordinaire, he asked if I'd seen the Brummell Report on top women on boards. After our lunch he followed up by forwarding the link. Excitedly looking down the list of the top women on the boards I found that I knew at least seven of them. I told myself, if all of the seven women I knew would agree to do an interview for me about their route to their boards, I would start writing the book. To my surprise all seven agreed, and the 7 Traits of Highly Successful Women on Boards was born. Word spread about the book and I was introduced to so many women, far too many for me to include in this book. However it was Hugh's injection that made me stop the theoretical and engage in the practical aspect of writing the book.

As the Radio 4 game show Just a Minute says, "Without hesitation, repetition, or deviation", I must thank Miriam González Durántez, of Decherts, for her foresight, knowledge and passion to cultivate women leaders of the future.

Thanks also to Fiona Woolf CBE, Lord Mayor, City of London for making a vital contribution to the diversity conversation during her term in office.

Lastly, to Mr Alpesh Patel, Senior Partner at EY for taking up the baton to put the spotlight on race equality in the boardroom in the years to come.

The group of people I would like to thank most of all are the real stars, the women themselves who took time out to share their stories, their thoughts, joys and fears. We sometimes forget that free time whilst working in a high-profile, highly-charged job is a rare commodity indeed. They are:

Andrea Wong - Sony Pictures; Antonia Belcher - MHBC; Baroness Jo Valentine - London First; Baroness Patience Wheatcroft - FIAT SpA; Beatriz Pessoa de Araujo - Baker & McKenzie; Carole Stone - YouGov-Cambridge; Claire Ighodaro CBE - Lloyds of London; Cornelia Meyer - Gasol; Dame Judith Mayhew Jonas - London & Partners; Davida Marston - Bank of Ireland; Fiona Cannon - Lloyds Banking Group; Fleur Bothwick OBE - EY; Heather Rabbatts CBE - The Football Association; Karen Blackett OBE - MediaCom; Kate Robertson – Havas Worldwide; Kirsten English - eFront; Melanie Richards - KPMG; Natalie Griffin - DWF; Paula Vennells - Post Office; Sharon Thorne - Deloitte; Sheekha Rajani - Diversity Jobs; Trusha Kachhela - PwC.

Despite me being unknown to some of these women they allowed me into their homes, their offices, their heads and their hearts, therefore it is my greatest wish that I, accurately, reflect what they shared with me.

Although the number of men interviewed for this book could have easily matched or outnumbered the women, I made a conscious decision to only interview three. Individually they have made considerable contributions to, and are helping to shape, the national conversation of Women on Boards. These men are David Cruickshank, Chairman of Deloitte, founder of Deloitte Academy's Women on Boards Programme and Patron of Inspiring the Future campaign, Sir John Parker, Patron of the 30% Club, and Lord Mervyn Davies whose "Women on Boards" report has provided the gender equality debate with much needed oxygen.

Last but never least, others whose guidance, knowledge and help made my task significantly easier include Baroness Howells of St David's for her astute and sound counsel over the years, the effervescent Mandy Jeffries at Deloitte; Ann Philip at Deloitte Academy; Morgan Lobb of Diversity Jobs; Sophie Chandauka of Virgin Money; Mindy Gibbins-Klein, Panoma Press and The Book Midwife; Dr Atul Shah; University Campus Suffolk; Niquitha Thompson, make-up and stylist, Misako Devereux; Photographer, Rona Gjokoli; Videographer, Danielle Osman; Videographer, Chantal Claricia; 7 Traits of Highly Successful Women on Boards – France, Maritza Russell; 7 Traits of Highly Successful Women on Boards – Netherlands. I could not possibly end without acknowledgments to Maya Angelou, the inspirational godmother to many women across the world, surpassing age and race, who passed away in May 2014. We owe her much.

Also to the unstoppable Oprah Winfrey, international inspirational guru to many across races, ages and sexes, I give thanks, for showing anything is possible if you put your mind to it.

Finally, I believe behind every good man is a woman who should have had his job, and behind this woman is a good man who ensured I got this job done! Thanks to my partner Patrick Lewis for keeping my head in the game, when laptop and hard drives decided to crash at the same time, losing text, video and sound, for being my coach and mentor along with my daugther, Cydnie Thompson, Editor, 7 Traits of Highly Successful Women on Boards – Germany. They were alongside me through a really nerve-racking but exciting time.

I thank you all for inspiration, trust, faith and for helping to prepare this book, a gift and guide for others on their way to the top.

FOREWORD

MIRIAM GONZÁLEZ DURÁNTEZ

THIS BOOK is what most women on their way to the top should have by their bedside table.

Women still face multiple obstacles in the work place on a daily basis - far too many when compared to their male colleagues. Many of those obstacles come from historical stereotypes that limit their aspirations from a very early age. Many also come from a generalised lack of 'self-confidence' whose root is probably also linked to those historical stereotypes.

As a result, while women represent more than half of all new university graduates and half of the workforce in the UK, there are still far too few women reaching the top of their chosen fields. Instead, women make up the majority of the lower paid workforce and the pay gap still exists.

Both men and women have the right to pursue their dreams, whatever they are. Is it really impossible for women to pursue their dreams? Is it impossible for us to 'have it all'? Are we condemned to 'not having it all' so that men could have it instead? The answer, of course, is that nobody, men or women, can have it all. Being realistic about the compromises that are required to achieve one's dreams and having the wisdom to see any obstacles in perspective is part of the formula for success.

In this book you are going to find the testimony of some brilliant and successful women who have gone through many ups and downs to get where they are. Their experiences, their choices, their challenges - and also their doubts and their fears - can be the best piece of advice for other women, not only for those who would like to emulate their careers and reach the board, but for any women, no matter their current situation, their background or their career. Success means different things to different women - but all women who have achieved their 'success' share a 'can-do attitude' in life.

Yvonne Thompson's book should be compulsory reading not only for women and young girls but also for men. She has managed to raise the voice of an amazing group of women who are extraordinary female role models. But there are many more out there, willing to make their voices heard, to tell you their experiences, to help you and to inspire you.

MIRIAM GONZÁLEZ DURÁNTEZ DURANTEZ LEADS THE INSPIRING WOMEN CAMPAIGN. FOR MORE INFORMATION ON THE INSPIRING WOMEN CAMPAIGN PLEASE SEE PAGE 306.

FOREWORD

FIONA WOOLF CBE
LORD MAYOR CITY OF LONDON 2013-2014

AS ONLY the second woman since 1189 to hold my position as the Lord Mayor of the City of London I believe I know a thing or two about gate-crashing the 'glass ceiling' in a male dominated environment! The world has changed significantly since I became the first female partner at my law firm, CMS, 30 years ago. But it has not changed fast enough, and we need to challenge traditional thinking and make sure far fewer women and people from diverse or disadvantaged backgrounds get left behind.

Over the years there has always been a moral case for inclusion, but today, thanks to the evidence base from institutions like Harvard, there is now a compelling business case which screams out that if you are going to have a high-performing team at your top table, that table had better have some women on it. In fact, the better the gender and diversity mix, the better the performance. A more diverse team provides fresher perspectives, drives innovation and promotes originality. This change will not happen overnight but we need to ensure that businesses employ a true meritocracy, so that the best succeed, regardless of gender, race, sexuality or ethnicity.

One of my main responsibilities, as the Lord Mayor of the City of London as it has been for centuries, is to represent, support and promote the businesses and residents in the City of London. Today, these businesses are mostly in the financial, professional and marine sectors. Dr Thompson's book could not be timelier as this year I launched my Power of Diversity initiative designed to harness the benefits of diversity in UK plc and widen the talent pool on which it depends, to sustain its success and to create a genuinely inclusive City.

This book by Dr Yvonne Thompson is not only essential reading for both women and men in executive pipelines in the corporate sector across the country, it is relevant for women everywhere who are considering an executive career as a practical tool of inspiration. Dr Thompson's book provides a rare glimpse into the world of those women who are at the vanguard of this social revolution. It captures their journeys, it promotes tips and pointers and more importantly, it illustrates women in powerful positions, whilst maintaining their femininity. I not only recommend this book as a woman and as a leader, I encourage you to read this book to make your teams more competitive against the backdrop of constant financial, market and global change.

ALDERMAN FIONA WOOLF C.B.E.
THE RT HON. THE LORD MAYOR OF LONDON (2013-2014)

FOREWORD

ALPESH PATEL
SENIOR PARTNER, EY

AS A Senior Partner at Ernst and Young, the global professional services firm, I recognise that in an increasingly global and seamless economy, making the best use of the talents of the whole workforce is more important than ever. As an entrepreneur I have recognised and experienced a simple truth, to be competitive and innovative in today's marketplace making use of a diverse workforce is not just the moral thing to do, it is a business imperative.

Over recent years there has been a seismic shift in behaviours and attitudes within the corporate private sector towards women occupying proportionately more places in the boardroom. This initiative has been nothing short of remarkable, given the scant representation of women on boards a few short years ago. Dr Yvonne Thompson's book brilliantly illustrates the trajectory of twenty-two business women currently on boards within the UK. Through her book we get a bird's eye view of their world. Not just the obstacles and the gender barriers they have had to negotiate, but how they overcame them and their resulting successes. Despite their different approaches, experiences and challenges, we learn that these pioneer business women all have one thing in common, that they are highly effective, they are good at what they do and they make a difference.

I am left inspired by Dr Thompson's book. Not only because of the women and the contribution of the 'few good men', but because it demonstrates social change of this magnitude is possible. However gender equality is the start of a much bigger diversity debate for corporate boards. Market leading businesses operating globally will increasingly recognise that a diverse range of views, experiences and perspectives lead to better creativity and more effective problem solving. Irrespective of whether companies are global or not, customers and the workforce of today are not homogenous; therefore diversity is key. Having senior leadership with diverse roots, experiences and cultures will assist with the appropriateness of their products and services and help in developing new services in those newer markets. On the inside, a diverse workforce and talent base will look towards leadership for role models as part of their commitment to the corporate world.

Given the relative success therefore in the gender equality conversation, I am inspired to lend my support to the widening of the debate on the diversity of boards because this will drive better business and better performance given the global economy in which we operate.

ALPESH PATEL
SENIOR PARTNER, EY

INTRODUCTION

LET'S BE clear from the start, successful women on boards have many more than seven traits to define their success, and yes, there is a lot of advice out there already, but what I've not seen on my travels are the personal stories behind the data that is about the ascent to the boardroom as told by the women themselves.

So I decided to go on a mission to get the other half of the story that has never been told; not corporate, but from the hearts, the souls and also the heads of women who have been there, done it, are still doing it, and are willing to share.

7 Traits of Highly Successful Women on Boards – Views from the top and how to get there is not academic research, it is not a thesis, nor is it a statistical report. It's an easy-to-read interview account of 22 brilliant women who have kindly agreed to share with me their stories: the peaks and troughs of their journeys to the top. They donated their stories, not to impress but to press upon women the world over that whilst getting to the top of the corporate ladder is tough, it is achievable.

This book is written in an accessible way specifically to enable the widening of participation of women and future leaders. It also aims to show, if these illustrious women can do it, it can be done by other women, given self-belief, the right preparation and a bundle of drive and determination to boot.

The time is right, the time is now. 'Carpe Diem' has never been more appropriate. Never before has the boardroom gender equality conversation been so in vogue. With more and more businesswomen gaining positions on FTSE boards, this book *7 Traits of Highly Successful Women on Boards* has another incentive as it offers high-profile women already on boards another platform to be at the vanguard of the gender equality debate.

During the process of writing this book I approached 22 very special women, at the pinnacle of their business environment, to share their views and experiences. By their involvement they distribute insight to others and inspire with their expertise, tips and advice. In doing so they will not only be supporting a variety of aspiring women on their journey to the top, they will be setting standards in corporate mobility and responsibility for the women coming behind them. They will also empower the men at the top who want to know what women really think about being on a board, and hopefully inspire chairmen to think more about widening diversity and participation, and not be haunted by the nemesis-like scepticism about what women can really bring to the table.

I remain very grateful to the women who gave their time, shared their experiences and wanted to contribute to a very important topic that is of interest to all stakeholders and to the world as part of social change.

My aim was to get a good balance of age range, which I feel I managed to do, covering from mid-30s to 60 and beyond. I also focused on getting a balance in race, which I did not achieve so well. My one disappointment was that, although I could find many women who wanted to contribute, it was very difficult finding women of colour who were in a position to contribute. When I did find a few, more than half of those that I approached declined the request. Very puzzling.

Whilst this was very disappointing, it also confirmed my fears that there are even fewer women of colour breaking through the triple whammy of the race, gender and boardroom barriers that they come up against.

It is encouraging that the "Women on Boards" report has facilitated a significant breakthrough in the gender strand of diversity, but there is a mountain still to climb as far as the race issue is concerned, and possibly other elements of the other diversity strands also need to be explored with regard to equality on boards.

7 Traits of Highly Successful Women on Boards will contribute to the shortening of the already smashed prediction of the 70-year time frame for gender equality in the boardroom mentioned by Lord Davies in his 2011 "Women on Boards" report. Thankfully the production of that report has spurred more women into action, showing that we are ambitious, we are confident, we do have the savvy, and we bring a very different approach and contribution to the table, showing the benefit of diversity in the boardroom. Whilst my personal position remains that the marketplace needs external stimuli to increase the rate and the pace of gender and racial equality in the boardroom, this book itself is not advocating the many positive discrimination legislations such as quotas, though it is better than the alternative of waiting between 50 and 70 years for equal status in the boardroom across the FTSE as a whole. I do support the recent call for quotas, as this is not being hailed as a permanent solution but one that allows the opportunity to jump start equal status or an agreed target within a given time frame, after which market forces will determine the end result. Quotas have been adopted in some central European countries such as Sweden and Norway, and despite them being relatively successful it is early days and we have still to see how the market settles. In his interview Lord Davies maintained that the threat of quotas acted more as a carrot than a stick, and it worked. Do we need to think about this in other areas of diversity?

What the *7 Traits of Highly Successful Women on Boards* attempts to achieve is to help give a better understanding of consistent personality traits that come out from the women on boards interviewed. These in turn are distilled into tips and nuggets of advice aimed at equipping women in the classrooms, colleges, universities, SMEs (small and medium enterprises), corporate companies and supply-chains across the country with the tools to break out of the "imposter syndrome", a phrase coined by clinical psychologists, Pauline R. Clance and Suzanne A. Imes, and so accurately described by Sheryl Sandberg in *Lean In*, showing them how to be as confident as their male counterparts, and empowering these women to invest in their own self-belief and self-development to apply for and do well in board positions. After all, you have to be in it to win it, and two of the most powerful tips I believe were given in this book were very simple ones: "don't take no personally" and "this too will pass".

The most interesting lesson I learned during the interviews from the women I spoke to was that they all had something in common. Without fail, they all wanted to share and to be understood. But also, as soon as the interview finished, they all asked the same question which is 'Was that okay?' This came from the most confident of the women as well as those who weren't as confident. I heard it from executives and non-executives, no matter what the company. They all wanted to know, "Is that what you wanted?" However, I don't recall that element of doubt from the men I interviewed for this book, none of whom asked the question, "Was that okay?" Does this stem from an instinctive self-reflection which is naturally inherent in women and, needless to say, a valuable tool?

7 Traits of Highly Successful Women on Boards is a set of stories shared by those who have been there and done it, and is therefore a potential road map, or guide, to help women with aspirations to corporate leadership in the boardroom along the way.

Although some organisations are very successful at scooping up those who are already on the journey, in the pipeline, or even in the marzipan layer, *7 Traits of Highly Successful Women on Boards* also serves as a call to action for more of corporate UK to continue to develop mechanisms that prepare such women for what to expect when they get to the boardroom, along with advice and tips and support mechanisms to help them stay there, and to make relevant and highly effective contributions to their companies.

I'm sure like many women whose "eyes are on the prize", they have worked for, earned and deserve the chance to take up that one spare chair at the boardroom table. This can be daunting. At first it may seem like it is a step too far, and in some cases, a dream of something out of their reach. However, women are closer now than ever to breaking through the glass ceiling and taking their well-deserved place at the boardroom table. However, during my interview with Lord Davies for this book he revealed that the progress made had surpassed his prediction for the FTSE 100, with only one company within the top 100 companies without at least one woman on its board, but this was scheduled to change by 2015. Lord Davies had expressed the wish for Women on Boards to be extended to the FTSE 350.

It is said that there is at least one book in everyone. After 32 years of championing women, minorities, and small business, it could be said that there are many books in me. However there is another component which stands alone as a contributing and motivating factor for me getting my experiences out of my head and down on paper: the timing of the ongoing and still growing dialogue about board equality.

I offer this book, this labour of love, as I am passionate about being able to help, inspire and enable women to shed the "imposter syndrome", believe in themselves, have the equality of ambition to take those first steps, making their journey to the top floor more tangible, more attainable and more equitable.

I want this book to not only contribute to development of a greater critical mass of the best female candidates for the job, from new and existing pipelines, but in addition, with help from the inspiring words of the women and men in this book, it should push more women forward through the marzipan layer, breaking through the "golden skirts", and the "old boys' networks". Thus it should bring forth a richer, more diverse talent pool of excelling minds, to represent the UK in the global markets they now operate within.

METHODOLOGY

IN ORDER to complete this book, over a 12 month period I interviewed 25 very special people, 22 women and three men. For the women on boards that I interviewed, they were all given the same questions which enabled them to provide me with their unique answers and experiences in their own inimitable style. The men interviewed went through a similar process but with a different set of questions to which to respond. The vast majority of the 25 people that I interviewed for this book I was able to meet in their work environment, and on their home turf, if you will. I found the interviewees and their respective companies very supportive in ensuring that we were well accommodated, as invariably I arrived with my entourage which included a stylist, camera crew and a photographer, ready to record! For the most part the interviews were carried out face-to-face, complete with my intrepid video crew. However, for those with packed schedules I had to make do by completing the interviews over the phone.

I encouraged all the interviewees to give as much or as little as they felt comfortable doing. The resulting interviews were anything between 20 minutes and an hour long.

With over 15 hours of audio and 10 hours of video tape, and many more hours of researching and transcribing, I was finally able to find a common thread through which to distil many of their personal traits in a format that could be easily digestible for this book. This thread I call the seven traits of L.E.A.D.E.R.S., which stands for: Leadership, Education, Advice, Diversity, Emotional Intelligence, Resilience and Sidebar. Sidebar is the section where our women on boards share an assortment of quirky and interesting behaviours, habits and attitudes that reinforce their femininity outside the boardroom, whilst enhancing their ability to perform as powerful women in the boardroom.

This book is not a data-driven research manual. Nor is it a book steeped in research tradition, surveys or polls. Nor is it a nod to all the scientific rationality that occurs in policy driven documentation. Rather, the *7 Traits of Highly Successful Women on Boards* refers to the experiences and the actual and factual testimonies from the mouths of the women that matter, a cross-section of different women at different levels of companies in and outside of the FTSE.

7 Traits of Highly Successful Women on Boards reveals the business-style and, in some cases, the lifestyle of those very rare creatures, the women who have broken the glass ceiling and who have dared to go beyond the senior management and into the world of the corporate executive and non–executive boardroom. *7 Traits of Highly Successful Women on Boards* also provides an insight into the minds of the women on boards today. In allowing me into their private worlds these business women generously share the challenges, the obstacles and the lessons learned on their journey to the top. In addition to freely providing advice, they offer their secret to attaining the most coveted positions for the professional business person. A place in the boardroom.

After spending much time with each of the women leaders, I felt best placed to be the arbitrator of which category of the acronym LEADERS each should be placed, and which top tips to include at the end of each chapter. The placing reflects my personal opinion of where and how they fit into the book, and does not reflect on any of their qualifications, experience or expertise in the matter of being on a board.

All interviews took place during 2013/2014. All information contained in this book was correct at the time of going to print, and represents personal, not company, opinions and policies.

METHODOLOGY

Before we begin

I HAVE had the distinct honour of interviewing 22 remarkable women and three remarkable men en route to writing this book about a subject matter that is very much in vogue, and having been there myself, one that is also close to my heart. Its relevance today is not only due to the efforts of the people who were interviewed for this book, it is largely due to the many people who have backed the various campaigns, carried out the many pieces of research, run government and private courses and workshops, started clubs, developed pipelines and networks and written many articles, reports and books. Whilst we are getting there, there is still a long way to go. Martin Luther King, Jr, famous orator and civil rights leader, had a dream "that black people be judged by the content of their character, not the colour of their skin". I too have a dream, that women be judged by the content of their character, the diversity of contributions they make, and not by their gender. This rings true for me especially as I want my granddaughter, as a citizen of Europe, to grow up "sans frontièrs" – mental, social or environmental – placed on her. None of these factors should determine how she will go about making her contribution to society, which could include leading a corporate boardroom.

Whilst I share it with you, this is not my story, these are not my advice tips, traits or characteristics. These are the stories of a mastermind group of women, as they have told them, from their points of view.

From these women I've heard stories from the heart; they've shared personal moments, from their greatest regrets to their most significant achievements, in order to help others achieve their dream in a shorter period of time than they have.

There is a lot of valuable information in this book. It is said that "information is power", but I would argue that it isn't the information, but rather *how* one uses it, that is powerful. So be my guest, and do your best.

WHO SHOULD READ THIS BOOK?

Any female regardless of age wanting to know more about what it takes to get to board level, stay there and make a valuable contribution to the company she may represent should read this book. It will also be of interest to women who are already on boards, to use as a gauge of what their peers do and how they are doing, gain ideas and add to their knowledge base and board-survival tool kit.

This book will also be of interest to men on boards; chairmen, and other male board members. It will give an insight as to how and what female board members think, what they think of their male counterparts, what they need from men, how they can add value for men – the diverse thinking and contributions they can bring to the boardroom, and their betterment of the company.

WHAT IS THIS BOOK FOR?

This book gives information, inspiration, insight, and shows that, given the right foundations of knowledge, gusto and focus, it is possible for women to attain positions in the corporate boardrooms.

WHY THIS BOOK?

This was one of the questions that I asked the women who agreed to take part in this book. They unanimously felt that knowledge is best acquired through real life case studies, and anything that can encourage and inspire women to take leadership roles would be a good thing.

You can read a lot of theory about things, but sharing the experiences of others motivates and builds confidence. You're not doing it alone; you can learn from the experiences of others.

I asked "Why is a book such as this needed?" Here are a few of the responses. (The full responses are available at the end of the book.)

Carole Stone: I really think adaptation and the attitude to your life can help if you read books like your book.

Claire Ighodaro: I think a book which encourages and gives opportunity to people is critical. People want to achieve, therefore sharing learning is critical, so all the ways we can share with others are useful and should be utilised. I think if this book does that, helps others, enables others to achieve their ambitions to be helpful and useful members of society, then it is a good thing.

Cornelia Meyer: I think it is important to inspire the next generation of women. I think for our generation it was still a bit harder. I do hope that in 20 years' time we won't need to talk about women or men on boards. Women or men somewhere, or minorities or majorities, we will truly have come to a more equitable society.

David Cruickshank: I think this is an area where there is no monopoly of wisdom. I know that from some of the work that we have done in the 30% Club where we have pooled a lot of information and a lot of research, there is great interest in organisations on what's working and what's not working because none of us has found any of the answers, so anything we can add to that body of research frankly is welcomed.

Davida Marston: I think there is an increasing awareness amongst women and young women that in order to succeed you need to understand the workplace, you need to understand the rules and you need to understand how to play the game to be effective, and I think to an extent that experiences of women like me are relevant and I don't take that for granted because I think there are a lot of similarities and there are also a lot of differences. I think your (earlier) question regarding social media is a very valid one. I actually believe, for example, on boards you need a variety of ages because social media is increasingly important and I think around the boardroom table most people of my generation don't understand the way it's being used. We may think we understand it but I don't think we truly do. So I think there are opportunities for younger people to go on boards that may have not been the case in my day, both executive and non-executive. I think there is a wealth of opportunity out there which hopefully other people may be able to give some insights to which you could incorporate in the book, which I think will be very useful to young women as they start out in their careers and some of the ones who are a little further along on the journey.

HOW TO USE THIS BOOK:

This book is designed to be used as you wish: either in short bursts, as you dip in and out, so it can be read whilst traveling, or you can take a weekend and go through the whole book in one or two sittings. You do not have to go through it in sequence, but can use it in any order of the acronym:

L: *Leadership,* **E:** *Education,* **A:** *Advice,* **D:** *Diversity,*
E: *Emotional Intelligence,* **R:** *Resilience,* **S:** *Sidebar.*

Each chapter contains featured interviews, overviews, and top tips relating the topic of each letter of the acronym.

You can either read it according to the women who most inspire or draw your attention or the subject matter that interests you most. For those of you already on a board, just read through to see how your answers might compare with your peers.

7 Traits of Highly Successful Women on Boards gave me the opportunity to talk to and hear about women at the top of their industries, profile them, and also gave me the opportunity to ask them some questions that many others would find it useful to know the answers to.

Note: there are pages at the end of each section and at the back of the book for you to note down the profiles, tips, advice and traits of role models you like best, and have ready to use when you you need to.

What I hope the most is that you enjoy it, learn from it, and share it with others.

A FEW GOOD MEN

This section refers to the three men that I approached to participate in this book. They were generous with their time and contributions. During the course of the interviews they granted me full access to find out their thoughts, tips and advice on the subject of 'women on boards'.

Now of course there are many more than a few good men at the sharp end of the gender equality in the boardroom conversation, however in my circle and throughout my research these names kept coming up: Lord Mervyn Davies, because of his tenacious crusade to bring about a social change that will improve corporate performance because of the more diverse composition of its boardroom; David Cruickshank because of his support for the 30% Club, his work with the 'Inspiring Young Women' programme, part of the 'Inspiring the Future' campaign, and also his unstinting leadership and championing of the Deloitte 'Women on Boards, Navigating the Boardroom' programme; and thirdly Sir John Parker who has a history of supporting women up the corporate ladder, long before the suggestion of women participating in the boardroom was fashionable. He not only mentored influential women but recruited many to board and committee positions where their influences are still being felt today. He is also a Patron of the 30% Club.

Although this is a book about tips and advice from women on boards to women wanting to get there, many of the women I interviewed stated that there have been men who supported, mentored or nurtured them on their way to the top, therefore having a male perspective on the women on boards agenda is not only prudent for the women reading this book considering a career in business, but also men considering the same route.

I've put 'a few good men' at the beginning of the book for no other reason than they have something different to contribute to the conversation. These men are working tirelessly across the landscape so that in the very near future women in the boardroom are not the exception to the rule, as they are now. Therefore we can benefit from thoughts, experience and knowledge from a male perspective. In addition, I wanted to give a nod to these men and show that I am not afraid of positive discrimination with planned obsolescence.

You can positively discriminate, as long as there is a planned switch-off point, and then let market forces dictate. So without further ado allow me to introduce you to:-

LORD DAVIES of ABERSOCH, CBE
AUTHOR OF WOMEN ON BOARDS REPORT

LORD DAVIES OF ABERSOCH, CBE

HAVING WRITTEN the "Women on Boards" report and being instrumental in setting up the 30% Club, Lord Davies was obviously a must on my list of men to interview. A direct and no nonsense attitude came over during this interview and it was the same approach that pushed this report to achieve the heights it has. Mervyn Davies' formal title is Lord Davies of Abersoch, CBE. He joined the House of Lords in the Labour Government under Prime Minister Gordon Brown as Minister for Small Business, Trade, and Infrastructure. Prior to that he served 12 years on the board as Chief Executive and Chairman of Standard Chartered, "which is a bank that really specialises in the emerging market". He continued, "My career really has been spent in Asia and the US and Europe. So I regard myself as very much a generalist businessman although I have a career in finance I served on boards such as Tesco and Diageo, you name it, both large and small companies."

However, what makes Lord Davies relevant to us is his unwavering commitment to the national gender equality conversation for 'Women on Boards' as the Chairman of the review into Women on Boards. "I got involved in this because when I worked in Asia I saw the power of women in business and I just realised that it was very different to what I'd experienced in my career in the UK. I've also been a great believer that if you're going to have high performing teams which is what I've always been involved in, you need lots of different people, lots of different thinkers, lots of people who have different skills. And the essence of a great team starts with yourself."

Lord Davies has held several senior positions in the private sector globally which include Chairman of Standard Chartered PLC. Vice Chairman and Partner at Corsair Capital and Non-Executive Chairman of PineBridge Investments. He is Senior Independent Director at Diageo, and Chair of the Advisory Board of Moelis and Co. Lord Davies was awarded a CBE for his services to the financial sector and the community in Hong Kong in June 2002 and is a JP in Hong Kong.

He continued, "If you know yourself and know what you're good at and bad at then you will put together a team with more different approaches and intellects. And I've always used the sporting analogy. If you play a sporting game, let's say football, and you've got eleven strikers, you're not necessarily going to win the game because you'll let goals in. If you've got eleven goalkeepers you're not going to score any goals. So I think the evidence is very clear from Harvard, from McKinsey, from Cranfield, that the more diverse the team is the better the performance. And that means the more women there are, the better gender mix there is, the better the performance."

Since the launch of the report Lord Davies has been engaged for more than 300 speeches on the subject of Women on Boards and the report, and feels that the tide has started to turn, and is making significant progress with the Women on Boards campaign. At the time of writing this book only one FTSE 100 company was still to accomplish recruiting a woman on their board, and that was at that time in the process of change. During my interview with Lord Davies, I congratulated him on doing such a sterling job, but mentioned that there is still more to do, as during my journey to find my mastermind group of women, I found that whilst it was difficult to find women on boards to interview, it was even harder to find women of colour on boards to interview. Were there any plans to look at this aspect of equality in the boardroom? His response was direct. "No, hold it. You can't mention something like race and colour and not mention minority men as well. Because it's just as bad on the minority male front as it is on the minority women front. So I think it's a big fundamental issue that companies need to think about and seriously consider."

Food for thought – what's after the 30% Club?

DAVID CRUICKSHANK
CHAIRMAN DELOITTE

DAVID CRUICKSHANK: CHAIRMAN DELOITTE

DAVID CRUICKSHANK is the second of the three good men. I first met David Cruickshank at Deloitte when the then Minister for Women Maria Miller was launching a report of women in business. After more than 30 years of campaigning on women, minority and small business issues, I arrive at events such as this organised in conjunction with the Government Equalities Office to find that I am still the "elephant in the room". A room full of men and women talking about equalities and I am the only black person present. As in most of these cases, I feel it is necessary to speak up, and point out that this elephant has a voice and a very loud one at that. After my intervention, David spoke with me during the networking session after the launch. It was there I found how passionate he is about equality and the campaigns that he is involved with, both inside and outside Deloitte.

David is the Chairman of the Board of Deloitte in the UK, a role he has held for seven years. He is also a Board Member of Deloitte's global organisation, Deloitte Touche Tohmatsu Limited (DTTL), which he has also held for seven years. David remains an instrumental figure within his company and beyond in the work he is doing around gender equality in the boardroom with two distinctive and successful initiatives.

This is what he had to say about his work. "I've been a partner here at Deloitte since 1988 and I'm a chartered accountant trained out of our Edinburgh office after leaving university in 1979, qualified in 1982, and moved to London and worked here ever since."

David offered, "The principal organisation I support around the gender equality conversation is the 30% Club where I was the founding chairman with a group of others. The 30% Club, as the name suggests, promotes ideally around 30% (which is not a quota, it's a target and ambition), of Women on Boards. The thinking behind that is there was something in having a core, a critical mass of women to make an impact on board decisions. The 30% is a proxy for that. We ourselves at Deloitte have 25% of our board seats in the UK held by women. We have good representation and we want to improve it. So the 30% Club promotes Women on Boards. It also talks about how to develop the pipelines of women coming through to Boards and shares materials between organisations on best practise on how people can more effectively develop women into senior roles including the Board.

The Deloitte Academy's Women on Boards Programme is something we started about three years ago to help prepare women for board roles generally, women who are holding executive roles in organisations but don't yet have main board positions on public companies or even larger private company boards. We thought when we started off with the programme of the materials we could use that we had, so information around what goes on in Remuneration Committees, Audit Committees, Risk Committees, right through to the softer areas of dealing with the Chairman and the CEO dealing with financial matters that we could share with cohorts of women as part of board readiness, and we are now onto our fourth cohort of women going through that. Each cohort we have had has about 20 to 25 people going through it. I think women come to the programme with differing levels of experience, some come with all the knowledge of what the programme can give to them, but frankly, I think the programme gives them confidence, what they know and what they don't know. I think for others there is a bit of a learning journey, but I think that's now firmly embedded in our suite of programmes and we'll keep running it for as long as there is a demand and there seems to be a high demand".

David wasn't quite finished there. "Inspiring the Future is a programme run by a charity called Education Employer Task Force of which I am the Chairman of Trustees. Inspiring the Future is a bit like a dating site where it matches up people who want to go to talk in schools about their jobs, their careers, with schools who want people to go in. We have a subset of Inspiring the Future called In-

A FEW GOOD MEN

spiring Women which is very much focussed on successful women in business, not-for-profit organisations and government going to talk in schools about what it was that made them successful, what their career paths were, what the barriers were, what the problems were and how they overcame those and it's been fabulously successful. I'm really, really proud of the charity and the efforts we made. Inspiring Women has only been going for about 6 months or so but the pick-up has been phenomenal."

His response, when asked whose responsibility he thinks it is to change the balance of women in the boardroom, was "It's primarily the Chairman's responsibility to increase women in the boardroom. The Chairman can set the tone and take the lead. It does need some support from the rest of the board and the rest of the organisation to achieve it, but the Chairman has to set the tone."

Well David certainly has taken on the campaign, and has had a huge impact on helping the campaign to increase gender equality in the boardroom.

SIR JOHN PARKER
CHAIRMAN ANGLO AMERICAN

SIR JOHN PARKER

LAST BUT not least is Sir John Parker, whose support and eagerness to give support to women on boards I can personally attest to. Having experienced being on one of the committees that Sir John chaired, I was always encouraged by his wish to ensure at least visible diversity in the sense of race and gender.

Sir John Parker is a British businessman. He is currently the Chairman of Anglo American PLC (the 4th largest mining group in the world) and Ombu Group, Deputy Chairman of DP World, and a Director of EADS and Carnival Corporation & plc. He is also President of the Royal Academy of Engineering, and a Visiting Fellow of the University of Oxford. Sir John has chaired five FTSE 100 companies, including National Grid plc from which he stood down in December 2011.

Asked what he considered the key issues that women have in transitioning to the boardroom, he responds, "Well I think it's to some extent like men. You have to get noticed for your contribution to the company and for your qualities. It's often tougher for women – because of the biological differences, if you decide to have children, you will have to go off to raise them. There will be a career interruption, and assuming the companies have good opportunities for re-entering the workplace, that's helpful and possible. But often they have to fight to get back in again. It's not a natural follow-up to bring them back and that's where corporates have to do a lot more. So women do have it tougher than men because of their career breaks. They are not here continuously – they get forgotten about, and that's where we are losing a lot of talent, at various levels in the company."

Over the years Sir John has been actively involved with the 30% Club. "It's a very good initiative, and before being involved in the 30% Club I was a member of Lord Davies' Committee that recommended the 25% women on boards aspirational target for 2015, and long before that was a champion of women in the boardroom.

I have recruited Maria Richter – she was on the Board of National Grid for several years whilst I was Chairman, and Anne Stephens, on the Board of Anglo American, engineer by training, and COO for Ford in South America and excellent board member and very inspirational."

For more information and in-depth interviews visit our website: **http://www.womenbusinessleaders.co.uk**

But first let's meet some of the women and see if they agree with our few good men.

WOMEN LEADERS ON BOARDS:
LISTED ALPHABETICALLY

"If you gather the collective wisdom of people who 'have made it' in life, you start to see a trend."

Oprah Winfrey.

The trend here is **LEADERS**.

Andrea Wong:
President of International Production for Sony Pictures Entertainment

Antonia (Toni) Belcher: *Director, MBHC*

Baroness Valentine:
Member, House of Lords, Chief Executive, London First

Baroness Wheatcroft:
Member, House of Lords, Non-Executive Director, Fiat SpA

Beatriz Araujo: *Partner, Baker & McKenzie*

Carole Stone: *Non-Executive Director, YouGov-Cambridge*

Claire Ighodaro CBE: *Non-Executive Director, Lloyds of London*

Cornelia Meyer: *Non-Executive Chairman, Gasol*

Dame Judith Mayhew Jonas:
Non-Executive Director, Chair, London & Partners

Davida Marston: *Non-Executive Director, Bank of Ireland*

Fiona Cannon:
Director of Diversity & Inclusion, Lloyds Banking Group

Fleur Bothwick OBE: *Director of Diversity & Inclusion, EY*

Heather Rabbatts CBE: *Director, The Football Association*

Karen Blackett OBE: *CEO, MediaCom*

Kate Robertson: *CEO, Havas Global*

Kirsten English: *Non-Executive Director, eFront*

Melanie Richards: *Vice Chair, KPMG*

Natalie Griffin: *Chief Operating Officer, DWF*

Paula Vennells: *Chief Executive, Post Office*

Sharon Thorne: *Managing Partner Regional Markets, Deloitte UK*

Sheekha Rajani: *Director, Diversity Jobs*

Trusha Kachhela: *Tax Partner, PwC*

Women leaders are like immigrants...

"They start from the outside looking in. They work twice as hard and twice as long to be accepted in the hallowed halls of the male bastion of the business arena, and all too often for the one spare chair."

Anonymous

Here's the story of a female immigrant who is still championing the fight for that one spare chair in the boardroom.

My parents, Richard and Edna Thompson, were the typical entrepreneurial immigrants. On the promise of a better life, they saved for airfares for two adults and six children to immigrate to the UK via the carrier BOAC (British Overseas Airways Corporation), now known as BA. We arrived in the UK from a little South American country called Guyana, which is situated at the northern tip of South America between Venezuela and Suriname. At that time is was still called British Guyana, not to be confused with French, or Dutch Guyana, both of which are still colonised. Having little money and nowhere to live, each child carried what was known then as a grip (a cardboard version of a suitcase), filled with as much clothing and belongings as they could carry.

It was an April morning I'll never forget, in what for me was a thick scary mist that tickled my throat and made me cough. I grew to learn it was fog.

With very little money in our pockets and thick, barely under-standable British Guyanese accents, we embarked on our adventure of a new life in Great Britain. I'd never seen snow, never felt such cold weather, and for sure never seen pea soup fog before.

Whilst staying with friends of my parents for a short period of time, Edna and Richard set out trying to find a place to live. It was at a time I recall when there were still notices on doors saying no cats, no dogs, no children, no Irish, no blacks!

Despite these challenges my parents still found a small two-room flat in a basement in Battersea, South London. It housed eight people for three or four years. Although I have had many addresses since, this is an address I will never forget.

50a St Joseph's Street, Battersea, SW11, is where I started life in the UK as a four year old. It is where I had my first taste of historical events occurring across the world, such as the Apollo moon landings and the assassinations of President Kennedy and Martin Luther King. All on our black and white Rediffusion television set. We were so poor, we all had to huddle around a paraffin heater, which was the same one my mother cooked on. For baths, my mother heated water in a metal bucket for each of us and carried it out to the hut in the back garden where she washed each of us, one by one, the boys first then the girls, all under the smog of Battersea Power Station flowing over where we lived.

We stayed at St Joseph's Street until we could move up, to a two-bedroom flat in Allfarthing Lane, Wandsworth, again in South London. St Joseph's Street no longer exists – the houses were so bad they knocked down the whole street. Today the location where we lived in Battersea, near the river, boasts a newly-refurbished Power Station and therefore a prime location for real estate development. Can you imagine what it is worth now?

In Georgetown, Guyana, my father held the position of Policeman which was a highly respected position within the city. On arrival here in the UK, in order to provide for the family, he took a job at St Thomas's Hospital as a plumber's mate, effectively down-grading his work aspirations of joining the Police Force in the UK. He stayed at St Thomas's as a plumber until he retired. My mother, the matriarchal epicentre of the family, was a wife, a mother to six children, a part-time cleaner and part-time machinist. Life was tough, however a strong work ethic was engrained into us by our parents. Given that we had little, our mother always found new ways to make what we had seem plentiful. Whilst being busy working she would find new ways for us to share things, new ways to prepare wholesome nutritious food, improvise on ways to clean the house. It really is true when they say that necessity is the root of entrepreneurialism because my mother embodied that as she improvised and nurtured in equal measure, and as a direct consequence of my mother's industry and work ethic, the entrepreneurial gene became part of my whole family's DNA.

After leaving school and trying a few jobs, I settled at CBS Records, a very male bastion, as an assistant regional Press Officer. This was where I honed my marketing and PR skills. Being the only black person who was not on the switchboard or a cleaner, it took seven and a half years before I realised that as a black person and secondly as a women, the only way to move up was to move out. It was then I decided that working for someone else was just not for me. If I wanted to get what I wanted out of life I had to work for myself. Over 30 years ago I started the first black-owned PR company in the UK, Positive Publicity.

Always entrepreneurial and very much interested in journalism, I freelanced for various lifestyle publications at IPC Magazines and also many of the music magazines at that time. I freelanced for the UK's first black monthly magazine, ROOT, which was where I was approached and asked to be a member of a group that started the first African and Caribbean radio station called Choice FM. This would lead me to become the sole woman on the board of ten people for over 15 years. I was a minority within a minority. My time at Choice

FM was littered with some fantastic memories and I was part of a social and cultural movement that was developing in front of our eyes across the UK. Eventually we sold Choice FM to Capital Radio and I never looked back. That station is now called Capital Xtra, owned by the UK's largest independent radio franchise – Global Radio.

Throughout my years I realised that I was lucky.

However, I did make my own luck as I worked damned hard to achieve what I did, but also made sure I gave back. Mentoring, supporting, advising, and coaching are part of my DNA. I've been on many committees, boards and charities, mostly not paid, but I found that being on some of those boards was better than being paid. I learned so much and did some the best networking ever.

In 2003 I was fortunate to receive a CBE on the Queen's birthday list. It was for services to the minority communities, women and small businesses, and in 2005 I was awarded a doctorate in mass communications and marketing.

I continue to contribute through various committees which I am still involved with, including mentoring and supporting students at the Greenwich School of Management, mentoring young Leaders on the Powerlist Leadership Mentoring Programme, in partnership with Deloitte, I'm in my third term on the Council for City and Guilds and on the Economic Honours Committee, where I launched a campaign to encourage more women and ethnic minorities to nominate each other for honours. In 2014 I was offered a further doctorate by Greenwich School of Management and their partner Plymouth University for my work in Business Enterprise and Global Diversity.

Today I am a proud grandparent of my beautiful granddaughter Katarina and will soon again be grandmother of an equally handsome grandson.

So to answer one of my own questions in this book – What are you most proud of? – the response includes: being the daughter of the best entrepreneurial role models I could possibly have, my parents, being a proud parent, a proud grandparent, having great relationships with my siblings (who incidentally are also entrepreneurs), having a successful relationship with my partner of many years, being a business owner, radio station owner, serial entrepreneur, recipient of a CBE, two doctorates, an Yvonne Thompson Day Declaration in Houston, Texas, being mentioned in the Congressional Hall, House of Representatives in the US, and in Hansard in the UK amongst others, and of course last but not least the author of this successful book.

I share this with you, not to impress you, but to impress upon you, that coming from my background, if I can make it to where I am, you can too. It just takes hard work, focus, dedication and passion in everything you do. Find out even more on:

www.msyvonnethompson.com

"As is a tale, so is life: not how long it is, but how good it is, is what matters."

Lucius Annaeus Seneca

LEADERSHIP

*"True leaders understand that leadership is
not about them but about those they serve.
It is not about exalting themselves but
about lifting others up."*

Sheri L. Dew

LEADERSHIP

IT'S OBVIOUS to all that women's roles in the family structure throughout history have been both as lynchpin and servant in most cultures. Moreover, in most cultures, matriarchal figures have also been the leaders of their families and communities. Women are no strangers to leadership – that is clear for most of us, despite statistics which would indicate otherwise. However, what we seem to forget is that there was a time when it was normal for women to be leaders in social, political and religious structures, regarded as among the most wise, honoured for their strength and esteemed for their power: biological and psychological facilities for creation and creativity. Furthermore, this equality was true for almost every culture.

We've all heard of Nefertiti, ruler of Egypt in the 14th century BC, but even before her, when Xerxes went to war against Greece (480-479 B.C.E.), Artemisia, female ruler of Halicarnassus, provided ships and aided Xerxes in defeating the Greeks and the Spartans in the naval battle of Salamis. And what of the ancient Amazon female warriors, not to mention European queens such as Isabelle de Castile, Catherine de Medici, Mary Tudor, and Elizabeth I?

There have been strong female leaders throughout history, and today we also have exceptional female leaders in all walks of life, but that is a relatively revived development and still not the common denominator. From a global perspective, the average woman is still viewed as relatively disempowered, inferior, subservient and having a secondary position (often called the second sex in some cultures).

The good news is that today's business world is primarily driven by profit. This means that the utilisation of expertise and optimal talent management take centre stage. Regardless of where you come from, your gender, sexual orientation or which social class you belong to, talent usually speaks louder than prejudice. If you have the ability to add value and ultimately help your company generate greater profits and productivity, you can make people sit up and take notice. And the means by which women leaders have done this are manifold.

There was a school of thought, particularly in the 1990s, that supported the idea of women being good leaders because of their 'softer', more communicative and loving approach to business. However, it is fair to say that this stereotype doesn't include the myriad of different leadership styles which women are bringing to the business arena. It would be better to evaluate each person according to her leadership skills as an individual, and take the best of what we learn from each of them for modelling great leadership in business.

Following are some examples of what many would consider to be women leaders at the top of their game. Through a consideration of their stories and perspectives, it is possible to come closer to defining what good leadership skills truly are.

PAULA VENNELLS
CEO POST OFFICE

PAULA VENNELLS

Leaders are rare beasts. They come in all shapes and sizes. There-fore, there is no archetypal physical trait that marks leaders out in a crowd. I know from my own experience that the role of leader is a lonely position to occupy, and the larger the responsibility, the stronger you need to be as a leader. Our first woman in business due to the sheer size and scale of her responsibility fits within the leader group of the L.E.A.D.E.R.S. trait of women on boards. I went to her offices for an interview and she didn't fail to impress.

Paula Vennells is in a position of being probably the most unique female CEO in the UK – why? Because she works for two organisations. One has been in existence for over 370 years – the Post Office, and the other has been around for centuries – The Church of England. Her first employer, the UK's Post Office, incorporates 11,800 post offices up and down the country, with approx. 55,000 staff. Unique is not the only adjective that I would use to describe Paula Vennells. A powerhouse of a woman in a petite and trim physique, she is one of the most fascinating people I have met on my extraordinary boardroom interviews journey. However any superlatives to describe her pale into insignificance when you find out the full extent of her industry. During the week as the CEO for the Post Office, one of the most male-dominated industries in the UK, Paula oversees an organisation that sells a range of products from mail products, parcels, government services including pensions and benefits, to leading-edge digital identity and biometric photography, finger printing and electronic signature capture. The list also includes current accounts, financial services, mortgages and a range of home services including telephony. At the moment the Post Office is funded to the tune of about £200 million in tax payers' subsidies and its mission is to become a commercial business whilst retaining the public purpose. The Post Office distributes about £80 billion worth of cash. Fourteen pence in every pound in the UK comes through a post office.

In describing how she started Paula mentions, "I came through a very, what I would say, normal commercial corporate channel. So I started off as a graduate trainee with Unilever. I worked for L'Oreal for a couple of years, partly because I wanted to use my languages as my degree was in interpreting. I'm multi-lingual with French and Russian. It was at L'Oreal where I got into, and continued, my career in marketing. I was a marketing director by the time I was 28, and if I look back, I hit the 'glass ceiling'. It wasn't until I was just over 50 that I finally became a managing director." Paula continued to explain, "In that intervening period I did a lot of very different commercial jobs. I was a sales director; I ran a supply chain; I was a group commercial director for Whitbread; I worked for a number of UK leisure and retail companies; so in a sense, the experience I have behind me has prepared me really well for this role. I became chief executive of the Post Office just under two years ago when we separated formally from Royal Mail Group."

However it is what Paula does in her other job that sets her apart from most CEOs, men included! "I'm also an ordained priest in the Church of England. So most weekends I take one or two services in one of three local churches, weddings, baptisms, occasionally funerals but I need to take leave for that, so not too many of those." Apart from the diverse nature of what she does, Paula can boast that she works for arguably two of the oldest institutions in the UK, each with huge constituencies.

For a formidable, powerful businesswoman Paula seems tremendously grounded. She goes on to add, "What's really important to me in life is my family. I'm married… we have two teenage sons who are just going through GCSEs and A Levels. When I'm not working at the Post Office I'm doing things with my family. To completely wind down I read and I cycle or run. When in season, I ski. So the things that are sort of important to me outside of work are family, faith and keeping fit."

I looked forward to finding out who Paula admired as a leader and why; what she thinks the essential traits and characteristics are for being on a board; what tips she could give to women aspiring to be on boards; and share with some of her peers what similarities there may be. So I did what all good interviewers do… I asked her.

LEADERS ADMIRED MOST?

"When I'm asked which two leaders I admire and why, there's always one comes to mind immediately and that person is Stanley Kalms. Stanley, now Lord Kalms, was the managing director and the chairman of Dixons Stores Group where I worked for five years. The thing that I remember most about Stanley is "How can you do it better?" So no matter how good a job you did it was always "How could you do it better?" So the thing I got from Stanley was to never be complacent."

Paula continued, "Margaret Thatcher is the second. What Thatcher did in the UK, women breaking into politics in a big way was a very, very big deal. I respected a lot of what she did; and I disagreed with a lot of what she did, as I think most people did. Recently Theresa May, again as a high-profile woman in politics having the courage which both of them demonstrated to take on what appeared to be difficult things. One much younger woman who I have never met but whose book just rang so many bells for me was Sheryl Sandberg. *Lean In* – really great book."

ESSENTIAL CHARACTERISTICS OF BEING ON A BOARD?

"I would say there are two," Paula added, "listening and impact: possibly listening even more than impact. What I mean by listening is, if you're an executive on a board which clearly as chief executive you are, you are gifted with, as in my case anyway, the most fantastic range of experienced individuals on the board and there is a tendency to want to tell them what a good job you and your colleagues are doing. They don't really want to know that; they can see that from the figures. Actually what most executives on boards need to do more of is to listen to the non-executives because they're there to make a really valuable contribution. And I think vice versa."

KEY LEADERSHIP TIPS?

"This would be coloured mostly by the seven years I just spent in the Post Office, so authenticity and perspective is a must. One is that whatever you are trying to do, and particularly here because the context is so broad in terms of dealing with Secretaries of State, Chief Secretary of the Treasury, trade union people, staff working in post offices, customers, you have to be authentic."

Paula has been in the position of dealing with union bosses and government during the week and at the weekends she is a curate with religious congregations, taking sermons, baptisms and marriages. This makes her tips on leadership from two very different perspectives both very interesting and very relevant.

LEADERSHIP

KATE ROBERTSON
GLOBAL PRESIDENT & UK GROUP CHAIRMAN
- HAVAS WORLDWIDE

KATE ROBERTSON

Being able to see beyond the immediate future is a key ingredient for a business person to have in a leadership role. Having vision enables you to anticipate new legislation, new trends, new markets, new skill requirements, and new opportunities. Our next businesswoman demonstrates her visionary skills and abilities by mobilising a generation, but before we get into this exciting piece of work let's introduce Kate Robertson.

Kate is both magnetic and persuasive in equal measure and the Global President and the UK Group Chairman of Havas Worldwide, which is a group of advertising, public relations and marketing companies around the world. She is thought to be the most senior woman in advertising in the world which is impressive, although, modest to a fault, she declares, "....these things are not unrelated to one's age". Kate has held a non-executive position at YouGovStone, and is UK Group Chairman of Havas Worldwide, where she has 60 CEOs reporting to her. The 60 CEOs run various combinations of the 13 companies which she took over six years ago.

Although Kate studied law in the University of Cape Town in South Africa, her first job after university was surprisingly not with a legal firm. She went to work at the country's first independent radio station. At the time she thought working in a radio station was cool and looked like more fun than the staid world of law and she was right. With all the partying and socialising that working at a radio station offered, Kate admitted that in those early years she did not take her career seriously, and like most young people at that time she had little idea of what she wanted to do in the future.

Whilst she enjoyed studying law, when the time came she felt she was fortunate to be able to change her career from law to the radio station and then into advertising. Over those early years Kate discovered that she was a people's person at heart and in a moment of clarity realised that any subsequent happiness at work was going to

LEADERSHIP

depend largely on communicating with and listening to people. Yet it was only when she got married, had a baby and became the sole provider for the family that it suddenly dawned on her that her job in advertising was indeed a career which she needed to take seriously.

Today Kate explains that if she had any regrets, her only one would be, "I wished that I had taken my work more seriously five years earlier". She added, "Maybe I would have done things differently. This is indicative of how seriously one does have to take one's career right from the start. Having a small person to support was a good focus."

As is the case for many of the women I spoke to, Kate felt she had a turbulent career. She recalls, "There were at least two companies where I could not ascend in the hierarchy. This either speaks to a system or my own ineptitude in getting myself promoted that I had to move companies a couple of times to get myself promoted."

Kate's views on male bosses were informative too. Her 11 years at Havas is the longest time Kate has spent at any company throughout her career. She commented that she felt "blessed in my tenure at Havas by having a very young boss", which she felt signalled a change in attitude. Kate went on to add, "I think I was lucky because at the time I joined I had a very young boss. My boss now is even younger than the one before." She continued, "Younger men have a different attitude toward women in business. Men my age might not agree, but that is my experience."

Kate is also a co-founder of the annual summit called 'One Young World' which CNN has dubbed 'the junior Davos', a testimony to Kate's energy, passion and engagement with the younger generation. Kate explains further that, "Registered as a charity in the UK, One Young World seeks to bring young leaders of the world together to network and make people like myself, leaders of companies, leaders of government, listen to their take on the changes to the world they want to make and want to bring about."

Quite rightly, Kate believes that we are in a time of revolution led by young people from all over the world because the next generation is truly a different animal. "These young people are digital natives and warriors. The reality with them is that they are connected in a way our age group never was. They have a very clear sense of the power that this gives them." She continues, "We are concerned about it in that it is disorganised power and that has been proven now, with the recent revolution in Egypt being an example. But it is power none the less. It is interesting work to be the incumbent leaders and to listen to the voices of change, for good and for ill, but to me that is incredibly exciting."

So with all of Kate's personal, corporate, and financial investment in future leaders through the One Young World charity, I was intrigued to discover which leaders inspired her and what characteristics in those leaders inspired her. I also wanted to find out who she most admired as she seems to have mostly men on her list of most admired – was this because she thought there is a difference between how men and women lead?

LEADERS ADMIRED MOST?

"In a broad sense Nelson Mandela and Desmond Tutu. The latter I know well. The former I never had the honour of meeting, but my daughter did have the privilege of shaking his hand. In business I am a big fan of some men at the top who are seeking to use their power to change their industries and to make the world a better place."

With her choices in mind I wanted to know more about what made her tick, and how she made those choices. Therefore, my next question was:

ESSENTIAL CHARACTERISTICS
OF BEING ON A BOARD?

"Business skill set. It does not always require a good understanding of the business – even if one were coming from a different sector, perhaps charity with particular skills set – knowledge of profit and loss imperatives and growth, and understanding what reporting actually means, and understanding the law around results and communicating.

Diligence. In understanding the company, its context, continually making a study of that business as if you were running your own is important. Some non-executives do that but not enough. This can be seen in some great non-execs such as Michael Rakes."

With her international and vast experience within the boardroom I asked Kate about her

KEY LEADERSHIP TIPS?

"Accepting that leadership can be for good or ill. It is the one thing that worries me because we don't teach leadership to young people. There is a huge lack of good leaders."

Kate has a very unique view of leadership. Her views on leadership are from a youthful perspective, for future leaders, giving incumbent leaders a view of what is to come. In addition to the One Young World organisation, Kate makes huge efforts to ensure ethical and authentic leadership traits and characteristics are instilled and embedded from an early age in our prospective leaders.

SHARON THORNE
MANAGING PARTNER REGIONAL MARKETS

SHARON THORNE

This woman was told that she would be wasting tax payers' money if she went to university. How wrong could they have been? Ironically, it turns out she is saving tax payers a heck of a lot of money every day of her working life.

Sharon Thorne is a member of the Deloitte UK executive and the Deloitte UK board (revenue FY13 £2.5bn). Sharon also sits on the Global Board of Deloitte Touche Tohmatsu (revenue FY13 $32.4bn) and is the Managing Partner – Regional Markets, having responsibility for Deloitte's services in their 17 offices outside London. Prior to this she led their regional audit practice for three years.

Sharon is a non-executive director and audit committee chairman of the CBI. She is also a trustee of Prostate Cancer UK (PCUK) and a member of its audit committee. She organised a skydive in 2010 for herself and three friends and raised over £100,000 for The Christie NHS Foundation Trust. In 2013, to try to improve on that, she took to stand-up comedy and as part of Funny Business NW raised over £130,000 for The Christie NHS Foundation Trust and Prostate Cancer UK.

After leaving university armed with the necessary qualifications, Sharon Thorne applied to Deloitte in their Manchester office. As a newlywed, her husband had been transferred to his company's office in Manchester and she obviously wanted to move with him. After being told there was nothing available in the Manchester office and never being one to take "no" for an answer, she applied again the very next day to see if there was any chance of getting into the Birmingham office.

Hearing of Sharon's determination, the HR manager at the time decided to take Sharon under her wing, championing her application to get her into the Manchester office, with eventual success. Manchester's smaller office meant Sharon was more visible thus enabling her to get more attention, support and a variety of opportunities early on in her career.

For Sharon, eventually ending up in Manchester and not London was pivotal in her career. She attempted to move overseas, but this wasn't possible due to the global recession. In her mind there was a clear-cut path to the top which included corporate finance for two years, but she was blindsided by a tempting offer and seconded to a client.

Having made that brave move and left Deloitte, Sharon quickly realized how lucky she was to have been there. "I was persuaded to come back to the firm in '94 but very clear by then I wanted to become a partner and had a lot of people supporting me."

There was to be another pivotal moment which would lead to Deloitte wanting her back. The partner in charge of the Deloitte office when she was there only ever saw her when she was submitting proposals and requests for money for social and sport activities. But a chance fifteen-minute meeting with him at an airport when she convinced him that she was far more than that changed her life for ever. He decided he wanted her back in Deloitte and the rest, as they say, is history.

Another defining moment was when she was on secondment in London in Deloitte's corporate finance operation and got to work with the person who was going to become the Chief Executive Officer, not that she knew that at the time. They were in a car on the way to a client and in that short drive she impressed him so much that he subsequently became her mentor, sponsor and supporter in her career. He has advocated her for various roles which kept enabling her to develop and move upward. He asked her to set up a young partners' advisory group where she became the chairman, and he also got her involved in UK strategy for Deloitte. As Sharon's mentor, he steered her towards a series of opportunities that lead to her getting on the board of Deloitte.

Sharon went on to become the first female on the Deloitte executive board as a managing partner in 2006, and again it was because of her mentor making a really bold statement to the firm that he wanted to get women onto their executive board. Sharon continued to carry out other roles which is why she is where she is today. She is also on the Deloitte global boards.

Being a leader at a leading company herself, I wanted to know who inspired Sharon as a leader and why.

LEADERS MOST ADMIRED?

"There are two leaders that I would say are very impressive all round. Two women who have had quite an impact on my life. They both have bits about them that I don't particularly respect, but also bits that I do. One is Margaret Thatcher and the other is Madonna. There is certainly a breadth of difference between the two. When I was growing up, Margaret Thatcher was a woman who came from nowhere in such a male-dominated world and was so strong. I remember thinking if she can achieve that, there is potential for other women. Again with Madonna, another woman in very much a man's world. She has achieved so much in her field and has basically done it her way and not thought about what other people think. There is something of that in both women. Worlds apart but in my eyes, great leaders in their own fields."

Given her breadth of opinion on who good leaders are, I also wanted to know what leadership characteristics she saw in them.

ESSENTIAL CHARACTERISTICS OF BEING ON A BOARD?

When I asked Sharon what she considers to be the most essential characteristics of being on a board, she says it has to be:

"Independence, courage and integrity, they are critical. Then breadth in technical competence and something to contribute to the conversation. Tact, diplomacy and communication are also essential in any corporate environment."

KEY LEADERSHIP TIPS?

"I believe very strongly that you should be yourself at work. Authenticity is critical – confidence and belief in who you are. Also, continue to improve, develop and be the best you can be every day."

Sharon has been with Deloitte since 1986, nearly 27 years. Her current husband is a brain surgeon. They have no children but Sharon feels that had she had children, she would not have progressed as far and as fast as she did.

OVERVIEW ON LEADERSHIP:

Leaders they admire most and leadership styles.

From Mahatma Gandhi and Winston Churchill to Martin Luther King, Nelson Mandela and Steve Jobs, there are as many ways to lead people as there are leaders. There is no right or wrong way – only the best way for the leader or the company. There are several leadership styles but the main ones are:

Autocrats are primarily concerned with tasks for which they're responsible. They believe the key is to focus less on subordinates and their needs and more on work-related issues. In doing so, they use their position to prescribe solutions and direct others to comply. This type of leader usually has more subordinates with low levels of job satisfaction than does the democratic leader. This is where most of the women interviewed agreed that leadership mistakes are made. Leaders that do not listen well don't include others and do not communicate well.

Transformational – which includes aspirational, inspirational, and creative, and is highly influenced by a personality behind the brand such as Apple, Dyson, Amazon, Facebook and Virgin. This is also sometimes described as 'Orchestral Leadership' – being able to create and lead a movement and bring it with you to the top.

Democratic leaders focus on their followers; looking after the welfare of their team is of great importance to them. They tend to be easily approachable, relationship-oriented and considerate of others' feelings. They prefer to lead by collaboration and empowerment. They're convinced that tasks will be better accomplished if they consider their subordinates' needs and encourage them to own a piece of the responsibility. These teammates tend to have high job satisfaction. This is the strand of leadership that most of the women on boards tend to lean towards, in order to get the right team around them and support them to the top. This can also be seen as bureaucratic, and doing everything by the book, but shared responsibility and glory seems to be the preferred way women lead.

As I wanted to share some inspiration with you, in this section I have looked at which leaders inspired these highly successful women, who they admire, who gave them inspiration on their way to the top, and who they might have modelled their leadership style on. It was interesting how many of them admired and were influenced by men, and / or women, current and past.

On the whole, the styles were mainly collaborative, collegiate, orchestral, and leading from the front, mostly democratic, and this is reflected many times by their choice of leadership role models.

WOMEN LEADERS:

The listings of women leaders our women on boards chose and why are as follows.

The women most admired by our women on boards started with Margaret Thatcher being cited by seven of the 22 women. Descriptions included strong, focused, knowing what she wanted, and where she wanted to take the country.

Next is Angela Merkel, three times described as a great leader, achieving what many other leaders could not achieve.

After her came Hillary Clinton for her drive, tenacity and strength.

Carolyn McCall of easyJet was mentioned twice – her vision as a leader and being able to move from a journalistic job to turning around one of the most entrepreneurial companies in our times, whilst running a home and three children, was described as truly inspirational.

Others mentioned were the Queen, cited for the length of time and the focus with which she has ruled this country.

And Malala Yousafzai as the youngest and described as a current and future leader.

Andrea Wong, Sony Pictures Entertainment: Mary Barra, CEO of General Motors, is one of the most impressive women I've come across. She has a very no-nonsense direct approach and it's very exciting to see a woman running a huge automotive company.

Beatriz Araujo, Baker & McKenzie: Margaret Thatcher, who I was inspired by at university, though I'm sure there are some strong things that will be said about that.

Carole Stone, YouGov-Cambridge: Carolyn McCall, who is the Chief Executive of easyJet – she moved from being a journalist in management at The Guardian newspaper and people thought why on earth has she gone to easyJet. She, with her board team, has managed to adapt and lead the company to where it is today. Diane Thompson, the Chief Executive of Camelot, had a rather sticky time when Richard Branson was about to take over the National Lottery licence and she fought and fought him on his own ground. She was very much a person in her own right who kept her feet firmly on the ground.

Davida Marston, Bank of Ireland: Angela Merkel, although she may be controversial, I think she inspires great loyalty in her people

LEADERSHIP

and you know what she stands for. Margaret Thatcher was an extraordinary leader, certainly for women, whether or not one agrees with the policies.

Fiona Cannon, Lloyds Banking Group: Hillary Clinton. And the reason for that is, I think, just her sheer tenacity. I mean, to be a woman in that environment. To keep going despite all the things that have gone on over there and at the same time to be an incredible supporter of women, I have to say, I've got a real bit of a sneaky soft spot for her. Obviously she's incredibly competent and the first woman Secretary of State and all those kinds of things. So a real leader and a real woman breaking down the barriers. And the very fact that she got so close to being the President of the United States. I mean "wow". I think that at the same time as bringing women within that whole constituency, and getting on because she's so aware of those issues. So Hillary Clinton is definitely somebody that I admire.

There's a woman within the organisation at Lloyd's at the moment who I think is a phenomenal leader. She's a regional director. Her name's Chrissy Quinn. She's regional director in our Halifax branch so she manages a whole region of branches. There are so very few women in those roles for a start. She's performing a real profit and loss business role, right at the cutting edge and the customer coalface if you like. But the reason why I admire her as a leader is she's got huge integrity; she's a great developer of people – that's her big thing. She surrounds herself with good people and she develops them and then they move on. Literally, I mean she's been in the organisation about 30 years and practically everybody senior who I know always says that "Chrissy Quinn was my first mentor". That's the kind of leadership I admire."

Fleur Bothwick OBE, EY: Angela Merkel, because we still struggle from a gender perspective in Germany. It is hierarchical, and status driven. So the fact is that she has retained a very powerful position and yet I, personally, have rarely read anything too personal about her. We don't hear about her hairdos, her outfits or whatever else, so she commands respect across the G20, across a group of very strong alpha-males. She is clearly highly respected and is clearly doing a good job, but for me, is all woman, so I admire her.

Carolyn McCall I met when she headed up The Guardian at the same time as she took on the chairmanship of Opportunity Now and that's how I got to know her. Mother of three children and, I want to say, twins. She then went on to easyJet, she's turned easyJet around, and again, all woman, fabulous to work with, strategic, engaged, and passionate.

Helena Morrissey is incredibly senior, influential, powerful and successful. She managed her family and has given back, and that's important to me as well. Helena with her 30% Club now chairs Opportunity Now and all the other fantastic things she has done.

Jo Valentine, London First: Aung San Suu Kyi which probably reflects where I come from and how rebellious I was at school.

Judith Mayhew Jonas, London & Partners: The Queen is the most extraordinary person. She's led this country for 60 years through the most extraordinary changes and yet has remained as relevant today as when she ascended the throne. When you look at her leadership of the Commonwealth and how important the Commonwealth is to emerging nations of this world, she is quite extraordinary.

Heather Rabbatts, Board member The Football Association: For leadership in terms of how people live their lives I always have to mention my mum who gave me such a huge amount of support. I still feel to this day her hand on my shoulder because one of the important characteristics of great or certainly good leadership is that those leaders who know who they are, who are grounded, are not looking to court being Mr or Miss Popular but understand that what you're trying to do is to be respected for your role in an organisation.

Karen Blackett, CEO MediaCom: Jane Ratcliffe, chairman of MediaCom and chief strategist of MediaCom. Sue Uniman. Diane Abbott. I remember in 1987 dad calling me and my sister to watch TV, when Diane was elected, and my dad telling me "if there's a black woman in parliament, you can achieve anything". Diane Abbott has not been afraid to stick to her principles, even when they are unpopular.

Kirsten English, eFront: Margaret Thatcher. She's a good old grammar school girl, and when I was going through the grammar school system, for me she was the icon of someone who had made it. I know she's generally commented on as being a great leader, and people have different opinions about her of course, but it's because she went through the same route as I did. You can see that someone has done it before, and I think that is very helpful because you know challenges can be overcome. The second leader is actually my granny. Sometimes you can look closer to home for your lessons. She ran a haulage business in Aberdeen and was a matriarch and managed to juggle a lot of things. She took me onto the staff at the age of eight and my job was to count out the lorry drivers' money, and she used to line up little brown envelopes with the amounts on them and I would take the money out of the biscuit tin and fill them. I had to stand and wait whilst the drivers counted their money to ensure it was right.

Melanie Richards, KPMG: Angela Merkel for sailing through two coalition governments and still being in power; given what's happened to all the other leaders around her that haven't survived. I have huge admiration for her consistency and calmness. The other is Malala Yousafzai, the young girl who famously survived an assassination attempt and has lived to tell the tale. She speaks with authority and authenticity. It's a bit of surprise to me when I thought of it – she is so young but I think she will go on to great things.

Natalie Griffin, DWF: Emily Pankhurst. I admire people who have the courage of their convictions and people who put others above themselves. Also, people like Dame Kelly Holmes who struggle through injury to achieve what they set their sights on. I admire them for their tenacity and dealing with adversity.

Patience Wheatcroft, FIAT: Mrs Thatcher. She was a woman who not everybody agreed with but she knew what she wanted to achieve. Very few people can say they changed the country but she geared the country towards the future.

Sheekha Rajani, Diversity Jobs: Lady Susan Rice formerly of Lloyds Banking Group has a much understated way of communicating. There were no obstacles too big for her; with sheer tenacity and force she tackled things, which was great.

Toni Belcher, MHBC: Maggie Thatcher. For the simple reason, she was a woman that was apparent at a time in my very formative career. It was a time when I was questioning myself and not trying to be too stereotypical about life but obviously when I was in my 20s and the role of women was very much different from what it is today. There was me, as a man thinking I would prefer to be a woman, watching what women were doing, and of course she couldn't fail to impress me. Apart from that I agreed with a lot of what she was doing.

MALE LEADERS

Men they admired, and why:

It was interesting to explore the men they admired, from Nelson Mandela to Bob Iger at Disney. The range of leadership styles was wide, but obviously worked for the situation and inspired the staff including the women I talked to.

Nelson Mandela was cited exactly the same number of times as Baroness Thatcher, which is interesting, though no one cited the two at the same time. There were no vast age ranges when it came to male role models, though the differences in the manner in which they led are vast in some cases, i.e. Nelson Mandela and Ronald Reagan. I was expecting to see Mahatma Gandhi, Martin Luther King, and even Richard Branson, Steve Jobs or Bill Gates

LEADERSHIP

for business mentioned somewhere in this list, but the outcomes are very interesting nonetheless.

Andrea Wong, Sony Pictures Entertainment: Bob Iger, CEO of Disney, is a tremendous leader. He's got great vision, an incredibly nice way about him and knows everyone's name no matter where you are in the company. He has a very accessible touch to him, he's incredibly smart and has lead the company very well.

Beatriz Araujo, Baker & McKenzie: Russell Baker, the founder of Baker & McKenzie – I thought he had a great vision, wanting to have a global offering that hadn't been available before. The chairmen are so different in terms of their leadership style. They taught me how to flex a lot under each of their leaderships. That was very interesting to me.

Claire Ighodaro, Lloyds of London: Nelson Mandela. There are a number of things in his life one could admire: his ability to learn right through his life, the things he changed, and how he developed, depending on where he was. The fact that he had such great humility – it is not often that leaders step down readily without being pushed. His efforts towards reconciliation and forgiveness at all times, even when it must have been difficult, I think are very good examples for all leaders.

Cornelia Meyer, Gasol: Jack Welsh, the iconic former Chief Executive Officer and Chairman of General Electric. Kofi Anan, the previous Secretary-General of the United Nations, is quite tough and you need a lot of diplomatic skills to get there.

Davida Marston, Bank of Ireland: Ronald Reagan defeating communism was a leader of his time and for these times, and I would probably cite him.

Fiona Cannon, Lloyds Banking Group: Our previous chairman, Sir Win Bischoff, has always been a huge supporter of gender equality. He was a founder member of the 30% Club for example. So, as soon as the Davies Report came out, he just went out and found his three women and brought them on board. Because what he was saying was, "Actually, if everybody is going to be after women, I want to make sure I've got the best ones". So he appointed three women pretty much straight away. So that kind of gave us our 25%, well it was 27% at that stage. But actually I think the real difference that it's made is, first of all, having those women on the board. This is actually because all of those women themselves are very actively involved in women's development and ask questions that maybe wouldn't necessarily have been asked otherwise. Also, because there's three of them, they have that voice rather than going into a group thing. They've been very influential internally in terms of the executive thinking about these issues. There is a very supportive internal attitude towards women, so they hold lunches, they're involved in all the role modelling programmes that we do. We also have really hands-on leadership from our three female non-exec directors and from our male non-exec directors. Having three women on our board has made a real difference. I think the other thing that it's probably done is that Lloyd's has just become the first FTSE 100 Company to make a public committment in terms of gender goals. So we've announced that we want to have women in 40% of our senior managerial roles by about 2020. I think having had the experience of a voluntary public goal on boards, although we hadn't directly introduced that, made it feel less of a threat to us because we knew that it would be OK from that perspective. So I think the women on boards stuff has started a real culture change. I mean – with Glencore now having the last FTSE board with no woman on it. Actually, when you think about what's been achieved it is pretty phenomenal."

Heather Rabbatts Board member, The Football Association: I'd have to say Nelson Mandela would be my first and foremost because I had the honour of meeting him when he came to Brixton when I was Chief Executive of Lambeth Council. What was just so overwhelming about him – and I know so much has been said – is that he managed to combine all of the attributes of great leadership with towering humanity. He was somebody that, whoever met him could only but be inspired by him. He would be my stand-out hero, beyond anybody else. I always find it's a very difficult question because leadership is forever changing.

Jo Valentine, London First: Nelson Mandela again shows where I come from and how rebellious I was at school.

Judith Mayhew Jonas, London & Partners: Lord Marshall, who was an outstanding corporate leader at British Airways and other companies. Moreover, he also gave an enormous amount back to the community in terms of education and economic development, particularly in London.

Karen Blackett, MediaCom: President Barack Obama, for his ability to transcend social class, and his ability to resonate and build empathy and talk in a common language about complex events and issues – also, how he can command a room.

Patience Wheatcroft, FIAT: Nelson Mandela. It's very difficult not to say, I've never met him but admire him hugely. One genuinely felt in the presence of someone extraordinary – very special. The effect he had in South Africa was remarkable, and what one admires most is his ability to forgive and just to concentrate on the moment.

Toni Belcher: Churchill, he's a man that came to the fore in a time of uncertainty when a country needed someone of that stature, someone of that strength, someone of that conviction, and they're all qualities that I admire. And I think he was a terrific leader in difficult times in the UK's history and he obviously made lots of uncomfortable decisions but he realised that they had to be made. I admire that.

Trusha Kachhela, PwC: Nelson Mandela for superbly rising above the barriers he faced, overcoming every challenge placed in his way, having that mental force and, because of what he did, he changed South Africa.

CONCLUSION:

The majority of the interviewees opted for male leaders as their role models in relation to leaders they admired.

Nelson Mandela was the highest quoted as most admired leader. Barack Obama, Ronald Reagan, Lord Marshall, Russell Baker of Baker & McKenzie, Lord Kalms of Dixons, Bob Iger of Disney, Jack Welsh, the iconic previous Chief Executive Officer and Chairman of General Electric, and Kofi Annan, previously Secretary General of the United Nations, also appeared on the list.

KEY LEADERSHIP TIPS YOU WOULD WANT TO PASS ON TO OTHER WOMEN?

Andrea Wong, Sony Pictures Entertainment: Hire the best people you can and empower them to do their job, and also encourage a culture of transparency, meaning everyone should be able to talk to each other and to feel safe about having any discussion that needs to happen.

Baroness Patience Wheatcroft, FIAT: Be very clear about what it is you want to achieve: if you are clear, people will follow. The majority of people like to be led. Be sure at all times you are ethical and behave in a way you would want others to – behave properly.

Beatriz Araujo, Baker & McKenzie: Be authentic, particularly because you need to build consensus effectively. You need to be genuine, people need to see you for who you are. Be resilient and do not take things personally and also be true to what your role is. Find out what is your particular role and stick to that.

Carole Stone, YouvGov-Cambridge: Remain focused, but also be inclusive of your team. You do have to make decisions. Sometimes the decisions can be right and sometimes they can be wrong, but people want leadership, they want you to make a decision.

Claire Ighodaro, Lloyds of London: 'Walk the talk', 'walk your own talk'. The most important thing you could do as a leader is to have integrity in these values and to actually demonstrate them. The second one is to be generous as a leader. Where you have experiences and learning that can enable others, share them. Be a mentor where you can. Be a coach where you can.

Cornelia Meyer, Gasol: The ability to carefully listen to key stakeholders in any situation, and the ability to persevere is always useful.

Davida Marston, Bank of Ireland: The ability to listen and then the wisdom and determination to take a decision is a must.

Fiona Cannon, Lloyds Banking Group: Always surround yourself with people who are cleverer than you because that is just always a brilliant thing to do. Take from the things that you admire about others that are good for nurturing and developing a talent. Make sure that you don't hold onto them, but make sure that they move on and be a real sponsor of talent.

Fleur Bothwick, EY: Take opportunities when they are presented. Research shows and anecdotally we know that women often stand back and reflect, like to weigh everything up, and like to be more considered. When I was offered this role, I said to the man offering it to me, "Oh I've only ever done Europe… I don't think I can do the whole job", and he said, "Fleur, we've reorganised, everyone has been offered new positions and we've all taken them. I've just taken one and I don't know what I'm doing, and if you don't take it someone else will do it and you will be working for them." That's a big turning point for me because of my role now. When I was a trustee for Working Families, the then Chair rang me and said, "I'm stepping down because I'm going into Parliament to work for Nick Clegg. We've looked at the board and come up with a couple of people that we would like to consider taking on the Chair and you are one of them." I immediately said, "Oh gosh, I couldn't possibly." He said, "I'll just ignore you saying that and let's talk through the pros and cons."

Heather Rabbatts, The FA: Two leadership tips that I would pass on are: first and foremost being yourself, being authentic. I think that if you try to pretend to be something that you are not, you will fail. And also you will never feel comfortable in that role. So I think being authentic is crucial. I think the second is to have resilience, to know that you may well lose many battles along the way. It's about learning from that experience. So I suppose I'd say the other attribute is to be resilient, but also to keep on learning as you develop your understanding of leadership.

Jo Valentine, London First: I don't think humour does any harm – you can get into sticky situations which can be lightened by a bit of humour. The other thing is integrity, it takes you a long way.

Judith Mayhew Jonas, London & Partners: Be confident in yourself and what you are doing because if you aren't confident in yourself, other people won't have confidence in you. Secondly, it is very important that women create strong teams around them who support them and go with them on their leadership journey.

Karen Blackett, MediaCom: The higher up you get, the more people will tell you what they think you want to hear, so surround yourself with people who will tell you the truth.

Kate Robertson, Havas Global: Nobody is the finished article. You need to trust your gut instinct. At the same time you need to be open to learning and listen to others.

Kirsten English, eFront: Understand your customers and be focused on business drivers that will help you become successful. Communicate well with people that you work with for your stakeholders and also your clients. The two angles of focus and discipline in the business, and wrapping your goals into communication people can follow, are vital things to have. Some of the greatest leaders do not know who they are. They have communicated internally, but not about themselves, which is the theme of the book *From Good to Great* by Jim Collins. Leaders have brought up teams and not been in the limelight themselves.

Melanie Richards, KPMG: The first is understanding who your stakeholders are. Once you've established who they are, learn how to communicate with them. Communication is absolutely key. The other thing that is very underrated is rehearsal. I am a great believer of rehearsal for all sorts of things. I think you can rehearse all sorts of conversations. We're used to rehearsing set pieces when we are presenting in front of large groups of people, but less likely to rehearse the critical one-to-one conversations. It's not about being contrived, it's about thinking about how to land your message and also to second guess the reaction that you might get.

Natalie Griffin, DWF: You don't have to be perfect. I think a lot of people think, 'I can't do that as I've not ticked every box.' You have lots of strengths – so know how to harness them and focus on what you can do, know what you can't do. Step back and reflect. You will be a different leader in each decade of your life from your 20s right through to your 50s and more. Be self-aware and know your capabilities, and keep pushing yourself. Never cry at work!

Sharon Thorne, Deloitte: I believe very strongly you should be yourself at work. Authenticity is critical – confidence and belief in who you are. Continually improve, develop and be the best you can be.

Sheekha Rajani, Diversity Jobs: The best way to summarise would be about emotional intelligence and the importance thereof, in terms of being able to lead and inspire as a leader. Being able to read signals and pick up on clues, also the importance of political savvy in an organisation, and having positive politics, are critical. You can't be blind to the politics that go on in organisations and need to learn how to navigate them to be successful.

Trusha Kachhcla, PwC: You don't have to change who you are. When I was effectively being coached for partner, I did not have as much belief in myself as everyone else did, and that became an issue. So what happened is that all the partners around me thought I could be a good partner but I did not get the position. I assumed I would have to change who I was to fit in. One partner said, "Don't change who you are, we want you for you. We want you as you are." My advice to other females looking to move up is – 'Don't feel that you have to change, but have real conviction and confidence in who you are.'

ESSENTIAL TRAITS FOR BEING ON A BOARD?

Apart from having the passion for the company, the knowledge of the industry and the drive to do the best you can for the progress of the company, you have to ensure you fit in with the board you are about to sit on. You need to research the chair, the members, their characteristics, and the personality of the board as a whole to ensure you adapt.

Below are some of the essential characteristics needed to be on a board as described by the women on boards and how they worked for them. This is what they said.

Andrea Wong, Sony Pictures Entertainment: It's different for every board as members will bring different traits to the board and that's what brings diversity. In other words, diversity of background *and* of opinions, so I guess it is important to be able to communicate what you are bringing to the table. And listening.

Claire Ighodaro, Lloyds of London: For me it's the three 'C's: Competence, Commitment and, most important of all, Character. Competence in that you have to be able to have the right skills, possess the right qualifications, the right experience and the right educational background for the role. There is no point going for a board role that you are not able to deliver on. So it is very important to have the right competences. Commitment is equally important because you have to have the resilience, the diligence and the capacity to contribute to the board. They do take up far more time than just attending board meetings. There is all the preparatory work for board meetings. There is getting the time to know the organisation and the sector you are working with, and there is understanding the people requirements, so it's a far broader role than just attending meetings. But the most important thing which really does resonate today, is character. And I say that because as a board member you should also have integrity and a strong ethical and moral framework, and you need to be able to stand up and be counted where there is a problem or a potential problem in an organisation. As a board member you are very well placed to challenge constructively and helpfully at the right point in time.

Cornelia Myer, Gasol: It is the ability to listen. Then the ability, together with the management and the other board members, to really create a vision and excite people to want to follow that vision and achieve great things.

Davida Marston, Bank of Ireland: Integrity, competence, which is not necessarily a given, and commitment. Too many people think that board positions are nice cushy part-time jobs, but they're not. And if you have more than one board, you can find yourself in a situation where crises can occur which can affect, crises or opportunities, such as a corporate transaction, which can require a great deal of time and commitment. Particularly if a company, for example, is floating, you can find that you are involved in all those daily board meetings and sometimes more than that. So you need to make sure you have the time available which goes to the point of commitment.

Fiona Cannon, Lloyds Banking Group: I think there are a number of essential characteristics for being on a board. The primary focus is about energy, commitment and motivation really. Because there's quite a lot of hard work being on a board. Lots of meetings. So you've really got to want to be there and be prepared to put the time and the effort into it. So that's really essential. Be prepared. It sounds obvious, but make sure you've read your papers and you have got something to say. Make a contribution. The other characteristics clearly are knowing your field and having a great depth of experience so that you can actually add real value. One of the more difficult things that I found when I first started on a board was the fact that you're not an executive any more, and actually sometimes that's quite hard. You have to move much more into coaching, making suggestions, posing the right questions, posing challenges, but you can't micro-manage because that's not your role. So the ability to step back and have some distance whilst also making a contribution is really vital.

Fleur Bothwick, EY: I guess it does depend on the board. There are some fundamentals which you need. If you have them, they give you great confidence. You should be able to read a P&L (profit and loss statement). You do need to understand the fundamentals of governance, what your actual role is and the importance of it. I've met a lot of board members who have happily signed up and totally overlooked just how important their role is if they are going to do it properly. You have to be able to think strategically – big picture… and then being able to relate that back operationally to how you are going to achieve what you want or need to. It's important to have an eye for detail. Also important is the ability to listen but also to influence, the ability to articulate your concerns, which we all do differently, and to get people to listen to you if you do have concerns.

Jo Valentine, London First: It depends on the style of the organisation and what phase of evolution it is in. I have been in very early start-up boards which have a different approach. You need to be able to take more risks depending on where you are going, as compared to an established board which means you have to be careful about strategy, investments, etc. Independence of thought is very important and also being able to work with others on the board. As one person on the board you have to be able to negotiate and persuade and bring people with you to come to joint decisions.

LEADERSHIP

Judith Mayhew Jonas, London & Partners: The most important characteristic or trait for being on a board is to know that you are part of a team, but it's very important to be able to distinguish between being an executive and a non-executive. It's also very important to be able to think strategically and have a vision and to enable others to follow that vision.

Karen Blackett, MediaCom: A natural characteristic of women on boards is their ability to be cooperative, and I think senior women leaders are naturally quite collaborative. They listen. You can't be thin skinned as there will be a number of times you will get knocked back and not be listened to.

Kirsten English, eFront: Focus, discipline and the method of communication is important. Everyone has their own unique style. So discipline, having goals and trying to achieve them are important. Appropriate communication is very important, and for the younger generations I would say that if you want to get something done, email won't do it. There's nothing like speaking to people.

Melanie Richards, KPMG: Being prepared for all the issues that will be discussed, what your role is and things you are responsible for. Also, be willing to express your view, even if sometimes it's not accepted – otherwise you are not carrying out the duties that your partners have asked you to undertake. The other area that is really important is to understand the business of the company and the company itself.

Natalie Griffin, DWF: The best leaders are the ones who don't put their own self-interest or their team's self-interest first. The ability to make tough decisions. Leaders are there to make tough decisions and best decisions on behalf of the firm, but they have to be the right ones. You have to be able to be challenged to do things differently, and challenged to do the right thing.

Patience Wheatcroft, FIAT: Have confidence in your own ability to ask questions – not that you will understand everything the company will be doing, but if you don't understand keep asking until you get the answers that make sense to you. Another essential is the ability to know when to say no. If you are a non-executive you must have confidence to question the executive decisions. So my advice if you have any doubts about any member of that team, they go or you go.

Sharon Thorne, Deloitte: Independence, courage and integrity are critical. A breadth and technical competence in something to contribute to the conversation. Tact and diplomacy and communication are also essential.

Sheekha Rajani, Diversity Jobs: Performance, impact and exposure model – you have to be able to be a high performer. You have to be able to collaborate, have gravitas, be a good communicator – and how you think about the bigger picture, how you influence change and affect progress.

Toni Belcher, MHBC: Firstly, I would say be yourself. I've always been myself even when it worked against me. There have been times in the past when people have said I'm too passionate or too emotive. But if you don't believe in what you're doing and that passion doesn't come through, then you're not being true to yourself. So it's very much be true to yourself.

Trusha Kachhela, Partner PwC: It's about having conviction, not being afraid to speak out. One of my personal development areas was that I was very deferential. As a director – the level below partner – the feedback I kept getting was that I was too deferential. I didn't get where I was coming from. So the firm invested in a coach for me who I worked with, and I work with her to this day. This was down to my culture. In my culture you have to be deferential. My mother is one of 12 in a very big family. So when we have get togethers we have a lot of aunts and uncles. When an elder talks they are right, even if they are not. I had no idea that I was bringing that behaviour into work, and clearly for work it wasn't the right thing to do. It wasn't until I was getting that feedback from a number of colleagues that I began to think why. So it was with the help of my coach that it came back to my culture. I realised that it was not about changing myself but emphasising a different part of me, and for me that gave me a lift. It's alright to be different at work – as opposed to not being different when I was growing up.

7 TOP LEADERS AS CHOSEN BY HIGHLY SUCCESSFUL WOMEN ON BOARDS

- ❖ Margaret Thatcher
- ❖ Nelson Mandela
- ❖ Carolyn McCall
- ❖ Hillary Clinton
- ❖ Angela Merkel
- ❖ Various own company directors
- ❖ Various family members

7 TOP LEADERSHIP TIPS FOR WOMEN

1 **Beatriz Araujo, Partner Baker & McKenzie:** Be authentic at all times, particularly because you need to build consensus effectively. If you don't, people will see right through you.

2 **Carole Stone, YouGov-Cambridge:** Remain focussed on your goal, but also be inclusive of your team. It's your team that will help you achieve your goals. No man or woman is an island.

3 **Claire Ighodaro CBE, Lloyds of London:** Be generous as a leader. Where you have experiences and learning that can enable others then share them.

4 **Fleur Bothwick, EY:** Take opportunities when presented. It is said – ask a man to do a job – if he can't, he will still say 'yeah, no problem. I can do it with my eyes closed'. He will take it and find out how, or worry about it after. Ask a woman to do a job she can't do – she will be honest and say 'I would love to but don't think I can'. She will therefore miss out on that opportunity.

LEADERS

5 **Judith Mayhew Jonas, London & Partners:** It is very important that women create strong teams around them who support them and go with them on their leadership journey. Let others know your goal – mostly they will help you achieve it.

6 **Natalie Griffin, DWF:** You don't have to be perfect. Don't think you have to be picture perfect on each task. It is just as important to deliver it as to procrastinate to get it perfect.

7 **Patience Wheatcroft, FIAT:** Be very clear about what it is you want to achieve. Keep focussed, stay the course, and you will achieve it.

TOP ESSENTIAL TRAITS & CHARACTERISTICS
OF HIGHLY SUCCESSFUL WOMEN ON BOARDS:

Great Leadership requires great 'followship'. Would people in your world follow you without question?

The real test of leadership is influence, and reputation; it's what people say about you when you leave the room. The women I have interviewed have described people they admire with various leadership qualities. Kate Robertson of Havas asked, "Can we teach leadership or are you a born leader?" According to our interviewees, if you are heading for the boardroom, some of the qualities or tools of the boardroom trade you need to have in your handbag should include credibility, confidence, sound communication skills, and the ability to effectively influence others to follow you where you need to go.

Over my 30 years in the diversity arena I have conducted keynotes and seminars on leadership. Throughout that time I've heard about what traits people want to see from leaders. Whilst there are a great many traits, from my knowledge, along with my interviewees from some of the UK's leading corporates, I've identified seven top traits needed in order to excel in the boardroom.

1   **Claire Ighorado, Lloyds of London:** Three C's. Competence, Commitment and most important of all, Character. This includes the competence of intelligence, commitment to ensure you put in all the time needed to respond to board papers intelligently, and the character of your convictions to stand up and be heard as necessary.

2   **Jo Valentine, London First:** Open-mindedness. It's hard to listen if your mind isn't open; or at least take time to acknowledge what is being said (whether you agree or not). This goes for anyone you're communicating with. To *gain* respect, you often have to first *show* respect. Start by being open-minded.

3   **Karen Blackett, MediaCom:** Listening skills. It's been said the average person listens to what you have to say only 25% of the time. With our busy lives, it's easy to not really listen. Listen closely and think before you speak. When you listen to others, they're more likely to listen to you. We have two ears and one mouth and we should use them in that order.

4   **Kate Robertson, Havas:** Vision. An integral part of leadership is first having a forward-looking vision and then being able to *communicate* that vision to inspire team members.

5   **Kirsten English, eFront:** Strong communication skills. Great communication is a base component skill within your leadership tool kit for achieving many goals. Without great communications you cannot tell people what you need them to do, when and sometimes even how. With it great goals can be achieved.

6   **Paula Vennells, Post Office:** Authenticity. You have to be authentic in everything you do especially if you are in a "people" industry. If not, you will soon be found out.

7 **Sharon Thorne, Deloitte**: Integrity. This is an integral trait for being on a board. Both work and personally. You will be judged by your integrity – your ability do what you say you'll do. People watch to see if your actions match your words. The minute you can't deliver on your promises, you are out of integrity and you lose credibility.

Here are two recommended Leadership assessment exercises:

1. Don Clark's Leadership Self Assessment Activity:

http://www.nwlink.com/~donclark/leader/survlead.html

Also widely used across industry this is a talent development tool to improve relationships, teamwork and develop leaders, among other things.

2. This Online Strengths Test will help you identify, develop and find the perfect combination of your Top Strengths.

High achievers:

- ❖ Spend most of their time in their areas of strength – they build their lives around developing their talents
- ❖ Have learned to delegate or partner with someone to tackle areas that are not strengths
- ❖ Apply their strengths to overcome obstacles
- ❖ Invent ways of capitalising on their strengths in new situations

© Noel Strengths Academy

To take the test and find out what your strengths and talents are and then build on them go to:

http://freestrengthstest.workuno.com/

LEADERSHIP NOTES PAGE

List 7 things you have learned and can implement on **Leadership**:

1 _____
_____
_____

2 _____
_____
_____

3 _____
_____
_____

4 _____
_____
_____

5 _____
_____
_____

6 _____
_____
_____

7 _____
_____
_____

LEADERS

EDUCATION

"You are educated. Your certification is in your chosen degree. You may think of it as the ticket to the good life. Let me ask you to think of an alternative. Think of it as your ticket to change the world."

Tom Brokaw

EDUCATION

THE VALUE of education in most societies has always been a focal point for members of social minorities endeavouring to surmount inequality and better their career opportunities. Indeed, for women in particular, this is truer today than ever before. In a UNESCO report on literacy in 2005, the average global gap between male and female literacy rates was 20% or over. But, particularly in Western cultures, women have come a long way.

In 2011, a survey showed that 57% of all university admissions in the UK were women, making men the minority. That being said, today's world is changing at a faster rate than ever before. What was relevant yesterday no longer applies as strictly today. For this reason, education has never been more essential. The question is, however, what do we define as education? Can we still regard traditional academic training as the best route to become educated? There is no doubt that, when applying for jobs, those applications which include degrees, master's degrees and doctorates will probably be more seriously considered than those without. Despite this, when one looks at the most successful individuals and entrepreneurs in the global business arena, many of them had no formal education or dropped out of university.

If this is true, why do we still regard education as essential? If you want to be successful, you need to be an expert, and expertise is gained through both experience and education. In addition, although you may never use most of what you learn in university, having a degree will give you leverage when applying for jobs. Once you have that job, educating yourself on your industry specifics and developments will ensure that you are positioned as an expert within your field. You will also not be left behind when the developments and changes of tomorrow replace what is held as true today.

There are some industries where this is more true than others, such as when an industry is highly impacted by technological advances. In these cases, educating yourself will mean the difference between stepping up the corporate ladder or being left behind. But in order to be part of the change, you also have to be aware of what is changing around you. This can only be achieved by training yourself in specialised information about your field, both old and new.

There is a certain amount of humility necessary for advancing up the corporate ladder, as those individuals who feel they know everything already and have nothing left to learn probably won't make the grade. However, those who sustain a balance between being an expert in their field and understanding that there is always more to learn will have a much better chance of rising through the corporate hierarchy.

In this book we see examples again and again of women who have continuously striven to grow, improve and develop every day.

Let's now look at how some of them have positively impacted their environment, both in the academic and corporate arenas, and what they do to keep at the forefront of their industry learning curve.

CLAIRE IGHODARO CBE
NED LLOYDS OF LONDON

CLAIRE IGHODARO CBE

Married with three daughters and three grandsons, tall, elegant and with a sparkling smile to match, Claire Ighodaro CBE is a Non-Executive Director at Lloyds of London. However, as I was soon to find out, her role at Lloyds of London was just a part of what Claire does. Claire's other contributions include chairing the Audit Committee at Lloyds in addition to serving on the boards of the Open University, British Council, Merrill Lynch International and the Lending Standards Board. As if this wasn't enough, Claire finds the time to be on the International Ethics Standards Board for Accountants, a body that oversees the ethical framework for over two and a half million accountants across the world.

Claire began her career at Otis Elevators, and later joined BT, progressing swiftly through the ranks. It was to no-one's surprise when Claire eventually became the Vice President of Finance for BT Openworld. Claire's rise continued, and in 2008 she was awarded a CBE by Her Majesty the Queen for services to business.

Speaking to Claire it was evident that she gives 100% to all the roles she participates in on the numerous boards that she sits on. To be able to balance all these requirements Claire would have to be disciplined, and Claire embodied discipline. I needed to understand where this innate self-control came from. As in most cases, the answer was in the detail.

Claire values education. In her own words she loved school as a kid. Looking back and laughing she admits that it was a little 'strange' that she liked school, but she understood what was required from her in school. Claire cites her parents' dedication for her educational appetite which is still firing on all cylinders today.

As I stated at the opening of this chapter, the educational trait that I identified in L.E.A.D.E.R.S. is not just based on the educational accomplishments acquired by the business woman to get her to the

LEADERS

boardroom. It is the constant striving and dedication to maintain their educational appetite throughout the machinations of the board and all its facets. In Claire's case, can you imagine the type of advanced training that she has to do to remain ahead of that learning curve that facilitates and implements training and development modules to service over 2.5million accountants world-wide? Throughout the interview I found Claire to have a very clear, some might even say clinical, view of what is required to perform in business at the highest level. Perhaps this could be best illustrated when I asked her what she considers are the essential characteristics for being on a board. Claire highlighted three C's: for Competence, Commitment and Character. Claire stressed that educational competence is but one of the attributes required to function on a board, and she maintained that you needed the right sets of experiences in which you acquire a broader skill-set to be effective. Moreover, Claire is very straight-talking when it comes to giving advice to school-leavers. To my question regarding what advice she would give to school-leavers wanting a career in business she responded, "I think some of the fundamentals are that you need to study, you need to look for experiences, so seek to get the best job experiences you can". To my question, what must she keep doing as a woman on a board, her reply was short, sweet and typically effective. "I hope to carry on learning until I am very old and wrinkly." Given this I have identified Claire as being in the Educational Trait of L.E.A.D.E.R.S.

Here is how Claire responded to some of my other questions.

WHAT DO YOU DO TO ENSURE YOU KEEP GROWING AS A LEADER?

Claire was straight to the point, "As a professional accountant I am required anyway to keep up with continuous professional development and I do that quite willingly… one has to stay in touch with developments there. I'm lucky, being a board member of an organisation such as Lloyds which is very committed, in fact, to keeping people at all levels educated and has a very good programme for its directors whereby we go in and learn what the important things are within our sector, within the industry. So I think learning is critical, but one has to have one's own development plan and stick to it."

WHAT BOOK ARE YOU READING?

"I tend to start books all over the place at the moment because there isn't enough time to get to the end of them. Because it's so topical at the moment, I've found that I haven't read Nelson Mandela's *Long Walk to Freedom*, so I've just ordered it yesterday, and I'm hoping that's the next book I read."

WHAT MISTAKES DO YOU WITNESS LEADERS MAKING MOST OFTEN?

"You know, I can't point to a single mistake that other leaders make, particularly because when I am learning I am looking for what they are doing right. So I have to say I am not a strong observer of the mistakes.

IF YOUR LIFE WAS A MASTERCLASS, WHAT LESSON WOULD IT BE?

"If anything is important to people I think it is hope. I would teach people to believe in hope and themselves."

We looked at education in the broadest sense, starting from the base that you would have the qualifications necessary for being on a board. But I wanted to know how these women keep up with the fast changing world in which we live. What I looked for is what additional learning these women did to ensure their continued growth as board members, be it lifelong learning opportunities, learning from colleagues, mentoring, coaching or industry based training. Let's see what the others said.

DAME JUDITH MAYHEW JONAS
CHAIRMAN LONDON & PARTNERS

DAME JUDITH MAYHEW JONAS

Dame Judith Mayhew Jonas is another of the women on boards that I have identified with a strong educational trait of L.E.A.D.E.R.S. Warm, adroit and very knowledgeable, Dame Judith is Chairman of the new West End Company, and London & Partners, both of which are small companies operating on the cusp of the public and private sectors. Dame Judith Mayhew Jonas DBE, to use her full title, is a British lawyer and academic. She serves on numerous boards of educational and cultural institutions. She was also the first female leader of the City of London and awarded the DBE in 2002 for her services to the City. Previously Chair of the Royal Opera House (and the first woman to occupy that position), Dame Judith has been Provost of King's College, Cambridge, and also chaired the London New York Dialogue and the British Dutch Dialogue. She has also served on a number of boards of educational and cultural institutions in recent years, including Birkbeck, University of London and Imperial College London. She remains on the board of Gresham College, is a Trustee of the Natural History Museum and a Vice President of London First, and was on the board of the London Development Agency. In 2004 she was made New Zealander of the Year in Britain and in 2008 she became Provost of Bishop Grosseteste University in Lincoln.

Dame Judith was born and educated in New Zealand. She graduated Master of Law from the University of Otago, where she lectured before moving to the UK as a lecturer in law at King's College London. Judith set up and became Director of the Anglo French Law Degree (Sorbonne), the first joint degree in Europe. She then entered private practice as an employment lawyer, rising to become Special Adviser to the Chairman at Clifford Chance, the world's largest law firm, before resigning to concentrate on her other roles. In 2006 she was appointed to the Board of Directors of Merrill Lynch.

Dame Judith's résumé is deeply impressive. I have had the pleasure of serving on a board with Dame Judith and I can attest to the great reservoir of knowledge, skills and experience that she brings with her to any facet of the board she operates on.

Education is obviously a big part of Dame Judith's life. She mentioned that even as a child she was focussed on what she wanted to do. "I think I probably began to know what I wanted to be from about the age of 15 when I decided that I wanted to be a lawyer, but prior to that at the age of ten I decided I wanted to leave New Zealand and live in London." It's quite clear that Dame Judith met the objectives she set herself in her formative years, however she cites her strong educational background and her training for her relatively hassle free career. Dame Judy comments, "I haven't so much had gender-related roadblocks in my career, I think that's partly because I was trained as a lawyer and that gives you quite sharp analytical skills and a can-do attitude and problem-solving..."

With education being such a dominant part of her knowledge base, I was eager to understand how a woman of such character keeps growing as a leader.

WHAT DO YOU DO TO ENSURE YOU KEEP GROWING AS A LEADER?

"My growth and development as a leader is something that I still regard as very important. I read the relevant books and magazines as well as interacting with peers on industry matters. Once you believe you have nothing left to learn, that is the day you should retire."

WHAT BOOK ARE YOU READING?

"I'm reading a book written by one of my close school friends called *Daughter of the Forest* by Juliet Marillier. She and I grew up in New Zealand on the other side of the world. We both immigrated to the UK and it's wonderful that one's school friends also make careers outside the country. It's really important as an immigrant to make a contribution to your new society."

WHAT MISTAKES DO YOU WITNESS LEADERS MAKING THE MOST?

"The biggest mistake leaders make, and this is often when they've been in power for a very long time, is they begin to believe their own rhetoric and their own propaganda and they can't be challenged because people are too frightened to tell them the reality. The emperor has no clothes."

IF YOUR LIFE WAS A MASTERCLASS, WHAT LESSON WOULD IT BE?

"Education can be the key to your world. Education and lifelong learning is important to me. I am drawn to constantly learning new things. It doesn't have to be in the traditional way of learning, but as I said before, if you think you have nothing left to learn you should retire."

Judith's position on learning has certainly served her well. Looking at the prestigious organisations and institutions whose boards she has been on is a testament to her philosophy on education. Definitely someone to learn from.

CORNELIA MEYER

NED GASOL

CORNELIA MEYER

As an international independent energy expert, Chairman and CEO of the MRL Corporation and media commentator, Cornelia Meyer is an example to everyone for her drive, but particularly for her ability to soak up knowledge which is the second aspect of the L.E.A.D.E.R.S. traits of Women on Boards. Proud of her heritage – "I am Swiss born, educated in Switzerland, the United Kingdom and Japan. In addition I am now a UK national and Swiss national" – Cornelia completed her doctorate at the University of Tokyo before she started her career, becoming advisor to Japan's Foreign Trade Minister. Cornelia then worked in several investment banks, leading functions in investment banking, banking and development banking. After that Cornelia was hired by General Electric and spent a good many years there before going over to BP as an executive in 2004. In 2008, working for the Kimberly-Clark Corporation, Cornelia became the Vice President Corporate Development, taking on the global responsibility for mergers, acquisitions, divestitures, competitor intelligence and in-licensing.

Today in her role as an independent management consultant she advises various multilateral and sovereign clients on energy economics, politics and fuel choice. Cornelia is currently a Non-Executive Director for Shale Plc and One Voice Europe, a Member on the Advisory Board of the Istanbul Finance Summit, a Panel Expert on Emerging Markets for CNN's programme Global Exchange and on the World Economic Forum's Global Agenda Council on Energy Security. She regularly appears on the media, including the BBC and Fox, as a commentator on business issues and speaks fluent German, French, Japanese and Italian. As she describes it, "I was a banker turned industrialist who now has her own company."

As someone with such a vast international perspective, speaker of seven languages, and an obvious flair for learning, I wanted her to share her thoughts on education for business.

WHAT DO YOU DO TO ENSURE YOU KEEP GROWING AS A LEADER?

"I read a lot of new books on this industry. I stay current in management techniques, in my own industry. I'm a member of the Oxford Energy Policy Club, the World Economic Forum, and the Global Agenda Councils. So I try to meet with my peer groups and learn from them."

WHAT BOOK ARE YOU READING?

"I am actually re-reading a book which is nothing to do with business although it has something to do with leadership I guess, by Dante Alighieri famous for "The Divine Comedy". It's just most wonderful to see how he looks at power structures and how nobody can take anything for granted. Even Popes end up in purgatory."

WHAT MISTAKES DO YOU WITNESS LEADERS MAKING MOST OFTEN?

"The inability to listen and the inability to communicate."

IF YOUR LIFE WAS A MASTERCLASS, WHAT LESSON WOULD IT BE?

"That even people you don't think can succeed, can succeed. Where there is breath there is life, where there is life – you can succeed."

EDUCATION

BARONESS PATIENCE WHEATCROFT
NED FIAT SpA

BARONESS PATIENCE WHEATCROFT

Her elegant poise, posture and graceful appearance is a definite hint that Baroness Patience Wheatcroft had spent some of her formative years in the arts. "I was determined to be a ballet dancer, and then I decided I wanted to be a journalist, because my feet were tired of ballet so I did decide early on. I went for an interview with the local newspaper when I was 17. They said go to university, so I did, and when I came out I became a journalist. I haven't wavered a lot from that. I spent most of my career in journalism largely writing about business and then I had the opportunity of seeing business from the inside rather than the outside."

With that kind of determination it is easy to see why Baroness Wheatcroft is in the Education group from my L.E.A.D.E.R.S. trait for Women on Boards.

Baroness Wheatcroft is a non-executive at Fiat SpA and St James's Place Capital, a member of Huawei Technologies UK advisory board and serves on the board of the British Museum. She is a former non-executive director at Wall Street Journal Europe, The Sunday Telegraph, and Business and City editor at The Times. Baroness Wheatcroft was also appointed by Mayor Johnson to head a forensic audit of the financial management at the London Development Agency and Greater London Authority.

Spending most of her career editing newspapers and as a journalist in both business and latterly in politics, Baroness Wheatcroft feels she was lucky to be invited into the House of Lords. She feels the two corporate boards and two advisory boards she sits on are very different but both very interesting. "It is wonderful to be involved in a business where real cars actually come off the production line at the end of it," she says, genuinely excited. Baroness Wheatcroft is also involved with two advisory boards – Bell Pottinger public relations business and Huawei Technologies, a Chinese telecommunications company which will take over the world.

EDUCATION

I was delighted when Patience Wheatcroft decided to do this interview. As I come from a background in media, which is seen as a male dominated industry, it is refreshing to hear a story of a woman who has progressed throughout the ranks and survived pretty much unscathed to tell the tale. Baroness Wheatcroft has made a career of working in male-dominated industries, and with her work in the car manufacturing sector, I was eager to hear who her main influencers were en route to the top, and what advice she would give to other women and future leaders about to embark on that journey.

WHAT DO YOU DO TO ENSURE YOU KEEP GROWING AS A LEADER?

"I learn as I go along. I consider myself lucky to be learning all the time. I'm not a great technology person, but with Huawei Technologies I have had to learn a lot about the various networks and things they produce, 4G, 5G, etc. One never stops watching what others do and trying to learn from them. If you stop trying to learn you might as well give up."

WHAT BOOK ARE YOU READING?

"*Long Walk To Freedom*. I just felt I wanted to know more about Nelson Mandela, his life, and what he was like as a leader… one of the best the world has ever seen."

MISTAKES LEADERS MAKE

"Short termism. There is still a drive to think short and deliver short-term benefits for shareholders. Leaders have to think long term."

MASTERCLASS OF LIFE

"It's never too late to learn, and can be enjoyable. I'm just learning about 4G and 5G. It's fascinating."

OVERVIEWS ON EDUCATION
LEARNING: WHAT ARE YOU DOING TO ENSURE YOU CONTINUE TO GROW AND DEVELOP AS A LEADER?

It was interesting to see the kind of learning that these women considered necessary to do to keep them ahead of the curve in their industries. Again, education does not necessarily mean academic, it's the kind of education or learning that keep you relevant.

Beatriz Araujo, Baker & McKenzie: Keep looking for challenges and stopping every so often and looking back and learning what you've achieved or what you might have done better. Look back and learn. I also have a coach/mentor that pushes me.

Carole Stone, YouGov-Cambridge: I suppose it is also always wanting to learn something new and not saying no, I already know that. I think there are different ways of learning. People say that I am known as a networker but I still go to other people who talk about networking and learn from them too. I belong to Cambridge Network and Cambridge Ahead, because I'm linked with Cambridge for the think-tank, and it's always good. I go to young people's events because it's very, very good to know what the trends are, and I always feel that there must be a very simple thing, the simple idea that could be good for mankind and still make a lot of money.

Cornelia Meyer, Gasol: I read a lot of new books on this industry. I stay current in management techniques, in my own industry. I'm a member of the Oxford Energy Policy Club, the World Economic Forum, and the Global Agenda Councils. So I try to meet with my peer groups and learn from them.

Davida Marston, Bank of Ireland: I think CPD (Continuous Professional Development) is absolutely essential. One of the greatest benefits over the last ten years as a non-exec has been in the time that I have had to be able to ensure that I do quite a bit of

CPD in a number of different areas, and part of that learning is not even so much the actual analytical work-related, it's learning from other people. So when I go to one of the auditing firms, specialist teaching for people on financial services boards for example, I find the views of my peer group as instructive as what's actually being told to us about the latest thinking or governance review, and I really do encourage anyone to incorporate CPD in their own lives, not just restricted to what they are learning at work.

Fiona Cannon, Lloyds Banking Group: Partly it's about watching the people that I'm really interested in and I see as doing great things, and talking to them about how they do things. So one of the things that's very important in any leadership role, certainly in the finance role, is about numbers, really understanding your data and all those kinds of things. It's not a great space for me because I'm much more over here with all the ideas stuff. So talking to someone, learning from someone who's really focused on data and that kind of stuff, that's a real thing. But also we have a number of development programmes here. So we have a 360° programme where we get constant feedback, both from our teams and from our peers, as well as my line manager. And using that information on a regular basis to hear and be developing constantly, rather than just one-off events, is the kind of stuff that I'm doing. Yeah. And for me it's "This too will pass". I find that very comforting when things are going really badly wrong, because you know that you've got to just keep at it, keep with it and you'll get through it. And of course it's a great leveller when things are going well. It stops you getting ahead of yourself and above yourself because "this too will pass".

Fleur Bothwick, EY: I continue to network a lot and I look forward to making new opportunities. Definitely I take lots of opportunities to learn. When I was co-chairing Working Families I wanted to better understand finances so I took myself off on a one-day, so there's formal training you can go and do and there's also a lot of informal learning you can do as well.

Jo Valentine, London First: I'm actually learning to speak Spanish. I think a little humility is important. So knowing that you never reach nirvana, and knowing that you have more to learn is an education in itself. I've done various courses including a wonderful one on Leadership. You go on a course for a whole week but only one little nugget sticks. Moving out of your comfort zone, like the first time I spoke at the House of Lords Chamber was a huge learning opportunity.

Heather Rabbatts, The Football Association: It's about listening to other people; it's learning from other people; it's learning by watching what other people do well, what they don't do well. It's about always feeling that you're never done. You're never done on this journey through life. Actually it is always about trying to learn something new every day – even when you don't realise it.

Karen Blackett, MediaCom: I have a performance coach who I have had for the past 10 years. I would count him as one of my cheer leaders who brings a lot of stimulus. I also put time in the diary for outside learning opportunities. The London Business Forum and their lectures are great. Exposure to people like Ken Blanchard or James Cracknell and just having those different areas of stimulus is really important. We use performance coach Adrian Green, ex-steeplechase runner. He is 'glass half full' all the time especially when I've had a bad day, he makes me see things in a different way which is really important.

Kate Robertson, Havas Worldwide: The advertising business has become more tough over the last 20 years, with revenue models in sharp decline and the coming of the digital revelation you've had no choice but to learn every day with the new waves that keep coming. In our industry you have to keep on your toes and keep running ahead of it. For me the blessing of One Young World which has made me acutely aware of young people, both there and at our organisation, keeps me in step with young people's expectations.

EDUCATION

Kirsten English, eFront: Most of my work now is in the context of boards. So there's quite a lot around boards, and financial services related to boards, especially as you need to know about all the regulations that pile in through that industry. You have to know about the regulations and framework. Part is self-learning where you need to go on courses about good boardroom governance and practise. You can also get mentoring or help from peers that have gone that way before. You can learn in their footsteps. A mentor recently said that every woman around a board table is a mouth and every man around that table expects something stupid to come out of that mouth. So your first words at your first board should be perfectly picked as that sets the scene for the rest.

Melanie Richards, KPMG: I read more, not necessarily a book. I embrace social media – where I am surprised at the efficiency of something like Twitter. I'm not a great tweeter – though I have hatched. I regard Twitter as a useful source of information. If you are following the right people, the snapshots and articles that you don't see on a day-to-day basis open your mind to different perspectives for sure. I put it in the reading category, but in an efficient way. I see that in a personal developmental context as well as reading books by interesting people who I think will broaden my mind and horizons. It is important. As you become more senior you can continue to seek feedback and act on it. Sometimes I do feedback from my end as to how I could have done things better. I also ask people I trust around me.

Natalie Griffiths, DWF: Take myself out of my comfort zone. Although I don't want to fix things that are not my personal strengths, I will on an annual basis do something that takes me out of my personal comfort zone. So if that's strengthening my presentations and adding to my tool kit, it's really useful. You can look back and know you've learnt something really useful from that learning.

Paula Vennells, The Post Office: I've had a coach on and off for the last 20 years. Not the same one. From a mentor point of view I tend to go and seek mentors around particular themes. So I don't have one specific mentor. I'll go and maybe talk to two or three people I know who've been through similar situations that I'm trying to work a way through.

Sharon Thorne, Deloitte: I do take time for self-reflection. I do have one person who I trust and who I can do that with. She is a coach, not a friend, not family, and not someone who I work with. She has a very high level of EQ (Emotional Intelligence) and being able to talk with someone like that and ask difficult questions forces me to look inward and helps me to develop the self-awareness I need to be a better leader. People always recommend books. I have been with Deloitte for 27 years and never feel that I have stood still. I'm always being given something new or asking for something new that keeps me developing.

Toni Belcher, MBHC: I read everything that I think I need to read, business wise, to be on top of the change that's going on. The change is the thing that will trip me up as everything is fast paced these days. I steer the path we take here effectively by trying to predict where the markets are going and what could be the next big thing and how the customer base is seeing us. I have to know what's good and what's bad for us. I tend to be on top of things and the only way to do that is by a lot of research.

Trusha Kachhela, PwC: I do a couple of things. I have an executive coach who is superb. We meet regularly, I can tell her my challenges and she can help me work them out. She is very different from me which is great because she takes me places I wouldn't naturally go. The other thing is self-analysis. There is not a day when I'm driving home when I ask myself if I could have done that differently. Coach is independent of the firm so I can get a very objective view, so I use her for more personal things. Mentor is a partner in the firm, I use him for more corporate things.

EDUCATION

WHAT BOOK ARE YOU READING RIGHT NOW?

Andrea Wong, Sony Pictures Entertainment: *I Stand Corrected* by Eden Galley.

Beatriz Araujo, Baker & McKenzie: *Transitions* by William Bridges, and a novel and sometimes a history book so I have two or three books on the go.

Carole Stone, YouGov-Cambridge: Richard, my husband, reads to me in bed and we've just finished reading *I Claudius*, also *The Unlikely Pilgrimage of Fry* by Rachael Joyce. Another book I read quite recently is called *Stoner*, by John Edward Williams.

Claire Ighodara, Lloyds of London: I tend to start books all over the place at the moment because there isn't enough time to get to the end of them. Because it's so topical at the moment, I've found that I haven't read Nelson Mandela's *Long Walk to Freedom*, so I've just ordered it yesterday, so I'm hoping that's the next book I read.

Cornelia Meyer, Gasol: I am actually re-reading a book which is nothing to do with business although it has something to do with leadership I guess. It's 13th-century Italian writer Dante Alighieri famous for *The Divine Comedy* and it's just most wonderful to see how he looks at power structures and how nobody can take anything for granted. Even Popes end up in purgatory.

Davida Martson, Bank of Ireland: Well I've just finished a very long book by Kate Atkinson who is one of my favourite authors called *Life After Life* which was really fascinating because it was a bit like a groundhog day. It's about someone who is repeatedly born in 1910 and has a different life each time, and it's particularly strong about a period during war-time, just pre and post war and what could have happened in different lives. I found it absolutely fascinating. But I do actually quite enjoy business books so my next book is *Citizen Quinn* which is about quite a famous Irish businessman who unfortunately got into some rather big financial difficulties during

LEADERS

the crisis in 2007/2008. I really enjoyed *Enron: The Smartest Guys in the Room*. The other books I enjoyed and are very well written were Gillian Tett's *Fools Gold*, and *Organising Genius* by Warren Bennis. I recommend both those books highly.

Heather Rabbatts, The Football Association: The most dangerous book. Tactitus's *Germania from Roman Empire to the Third Reich*.

Fiona Cannon, Lloyds Banking Group: Hillary Clinton's *Hard Choices*.

Fleur Bothwick, EY: The two that are open and on the go, one's on a Kindle and I'm quarter of the way through both. One is *Quiet* by Susan Cain, it's all about introverts and how powerful they can be, and again back to this whole theme of he who shouts loudest normally gets heard. And the other is *The 30 Lies About Money* by Peter Koenig, I heard him speaking. I have to say the book is not proving to be as interesting as his speech; his whole thing is try to think differently and don't be a hostage to money.

Jo Valentine, London First: *The Snow Geese* by William Fiennes.

Judith Mayhew Jonas, London & Partners: I'm reading right now a book written by one of my close school friends called *Daughter of the Forest* by Juliet Marillier. She and I grew up in New Zealand on the other side of the world. We both emigrated and it's wonderful that one's school friends also make careers outside the country. It's really important as an immigrant to make a contribution to your new society.

Karen Blackett, MediaCom: Children's stories – right now. I recently re-read *The Pirate Inside* by Adam Morgan, about trying to ensure that you should remain entrepreneurial even when you become a big company. The other one is *Tell The Truth* by Sue Unerman, the one written by our Chief Strategist about brand authenticity. Information for individuals as well as a brand.

EDUCATION

Kate Robertson, Havas Worldwide: Ploughing through an old Elizabeth Jane Howard, it's comfort reading. I'm always reading David Balducci; also reading Helen Dunmore, *The Lie.*

Kirsten English, eFront: *How to Build a Habitable Planet* by Charles H. Longmuir and Wally Broecker.

Melanie Richards, KPMG: *The Value of Difference* by Binna Kandola.

Natalie Griffiths, DWF: *The Kite Runner*, Khaled Hosseini.

Patience Wheatcroft, FIAT: *Long Walk To Freedom*, Nelson Mandela.

Paula Vennells, The Post Office: *Leading at the Edge: Leadership Lessons from the Extraordinary Saga of Shackleton's Antarctic Expedition* by Dennis N. T. Perkins, Margaret P. Holtman, Paul R. Kessler, Catherine Mccarthy.

Sharon Thorne, Deloitte: The book of the moment is *The Chimp Paradox* by Dr Steve Peters. He is the sports psychologist who helped the British Cycling Team and in particular Sir Chris Hoy and Victoria Pendleton. He has been helping Ronnie O'Sullivan and more recently Stephen Gerrard and the Liverpool team. He also went to Brazil with the England team, but that was a bridge too far! It has some great insights for managing your emotions, sorting out that negative voice in your head and achieving your goals. It helps in business and at home!

Sheekha Rajani, Diversity Jobs: *The Girl Who Kicked the Hornet's Nest*, Stieg Larsson. I love a good thriller.

Toni Belcher, MBHC: *The Hare with Amber Eyes* by Edmund de Waal.

Trusha Kachhela, PwC: *The Little Coffee Shop of Kabul*, Deborah Rodriquez. Females in Afghanistan coming together and being best friends.

LEADERS

ONE MISTAKE YOU WITNESS LEADERS MAKING MORE FREQUENTLY THAN OTHERS?

Andrea Wong, Sony Pictures Entertainment: Not making decisions. Don't fear making decisions, you are holding the business back if you think you are not part of the decision making. You will make mistakes, but it's OK.

Beatriz Araujo, Baker & McKenzie: Leaders communicate a lot because in their role they have to be careful what and how they communicate. The other side of the coin is to listen to what customers and the company is telling you.

Carole Stone, YouGov-Cambridge: What is bad in a leader is when you dither. You can't afford to dither. Take advice, make that decision.

Cornelia Meyer, Gasol: The inability to listen and the inability to communicate.

Davida Marston, Bank of Ireland: Not listening and believing that their way is the only way.

Heather Rabbatts, The Football Association: Usually trying to pretend to be something they're not.

Fleur Bothwick, EY: The biggie is not getting everyone's perspective. So being taken along in the rush of the 3-hour board meeting, trying to get through the agenda, watching the clock and actually missing gems. You know, make an effort, talk to people beforehand about the agenda if needs be, but always make sure that you invite feedback.

Karen Blackett, MediaCom: Indecisiveness. I think the wrong decision is better than no decision. People need to know where you are heading and nailing your mask. They need to know this is what we are doing. It is better than indecisiveness. You can always correct the wrong decision.

EDUCATION

Kate Robertson, Havas Worldwide: There's a lack of honesty and total transparency around the politics of leadership. In business everybody pretends, men especially, that there's not really any politics in the boardroom and around leadership. I see a lot of stuff going on masked with business rationale – when really you are dealing with something entirely political, personal and even emotional. There is a problem around that and I see it a lot in other companies.

Kirsten English, eFront: The essence of good business is being in touch with your customers. Some leaders lose sight of the reason they are there. So they forgot to be real.

Melanie Richards, KPMG: Communication. People know when leaders are not being authentic, when they don't believe what they are saying or do not have a strong sense of direction or purpose. The leaders, if they can't convey authenticity – it's a real challenge.

Natalie Griffin, DWF: Communication. The higher you get the more people want to talk to you or understand your strategy. People can't help but feel a bit more removed as a business grows. So it is important to keep people engaged by having balanced communications. Don't overload on communication as people will not even have time to read it.

Paula Vennells, The Post Office: Jumping to conclusions potentially without fact. This is a people business, and in relation to people it's either doubting people's ability to do something without any particular reason or actually trusting too much on the other side as well. Trust is fantastic, but you do also have to check that there is the detail behind it.

Sharon Thorne, Deloitte: Lots of leaders are guilty of failing to listen. Mostly from time pressure, they don't really listen to what people are saying and are not reading the mood music around the board.

Sheekha Rajani, Diversity Jobs: Sometimes when you come up the ladder it can be very easy to get caught up in the details. You have people there you can rely on, you are there to lead and inspire, don't get caught up in detail as it is not your place. Have faith in your team.

Toni Belcher, MHBC: Prejudging a situation. That assuming, or presuming, without facts happens a lot. I think also not properly understanding the reading papers, and sometimes they're too busy and they don't have the time, but when someone comes to a board meeting and is not as well prepared as they should be, and they do it too much, then people start to recognise that they're not really concentrating properly.

Trusha Kachhela, PwC: From a male's perspective, they tend to be afraid to ask females what they perceive as difficult questions such as what are their aspirations, especially those who have just come back from maternity leave. They feel they can't ask them about what they want to achieve in their careers. This is a huge mistake, particularly when you have women who don't say and men who don't ask – what will you get? Nothing!

MASTERCLASS: WHAT LESSON WOULD YOU BE?

One of the most important things I've learned throughout my journey is that how you see yourself is just as important as how others see you. This is a case of, "Does your internal branding match up to your external branding?" So I was interested in hearing, from my boardroom interviews, how they saw themselves and what they perceived others could learn from them and their journeys. These are the answers to the question, "If your life was a masterclass, what lesson could you be?" I called it my Oprah question.

Andrea Wong, Sony Pictures Entertainment: Resilience, and understand that life is the long game.

Beatriz Araujo, Baker & McKenzie: You only get one crack at it, so make every day count. Keep a perspective on both personal and working life. Be grateful; I certainly am.

Carole Stone, YouGov-Cambridge: My lesson would be networking, but the overall umbrella would be just talk to each other.

Cornelia Meyer, Gasol: That even people you don't think can succeed, can succeed.

Davida Marston, Bank of Ireland: Doing it my way. That's probably the best I can say.

Fleur Bothwick, EY: Resilience. I don't know how I would teach it but that's what it would be.

Heather Rabbatts, The Football Association: It's about where courage comes from. It's about when you look back at your life, at the time you might not have quite realised it, but why sometimes standing up against the odds or having courage because it's about not just going down the route of least resistance. So I would be a masterclass that talks about courage for leaders.

Jo Valentine, London First: How to be more open minded.

Judith Mayhew Jonas, London & Partners: Any masterclass that came from my life would be you can succeed.

Karen Blackett, MediaCom: Resilience. Anyone who has not had difficulty or been knocked back has had an incredibly charmed life.

Kate Robertson, Havas Worldwide: Determination.

Kirsten English, eFront: I'd like to think every bar I set I have eventually reached, and I hope to go on to find new bars, determination, aspiration and hard work. To all the girls out there, when you do all those things you must not do other things.

Melanie Richards, KPMG: Give your best and all to everything you are doing whether or not you are enjoying it. Embrace life.

Natalie Griffin, DWF: Believe in yourself and go for it. Don't look back and wonder if. If you try, you can at least say you gave it a go.

Patience Wheatcroft, FIAT SpA: Family comes first.

Paula Vennells, The Post Office: I would teach to never say no which is one thing I got from my father. Pushing the boundaries, courage, tenacity, and resilience.

Sharon Thorne, Deloitte: I'm a good lesson in positive thinking, positive emotions. You chose how you feel, you allow yourself to feel the emotions you feel, so feel positive.

Sheekha Rajani, Diversity Jobs: How to be a Libran. Sometimes leap first and worry about it later, don't over agonise everything, say yes and worry about it later. I think I have missed opportunities by over analysing. Just go with your gut; OK not to have done all of your analysis every time.

Toni Belcher, MHBC: Nothing's impossible!

Trusha Kachhela, PwC: Whatever your background, wherever you are from, you can achieve your ambition.

The information I got from this masterclass is that the women interviewed are very positive in their outlook about life in general. The steer that comes out in answer to this question is positivity, longevity, resilience, self-belief, communication, it's OK to make mistakes as long as you learn from them, collaboration and networking.

These seem to be skills and traits that come naturally to women, so to add my voice to those pieces of advice is to "just do it", and "Nothing is impossible if you believe you can."

BOOKS LEADERS READ:

I've listed all the books here as the range is really quite interesting from a business, leadership, de-stressing, educational or just plain enjoyment perspective.

Andrea Wong, Sony Pictures Entertainment: *I Stand Corrected*, by Eden Galley.

Beatriz Araujo, Baker & McKenzie: *Transitions* by William Bridges.

EDUCATION

Carole Stone, YouGov-Cambridge: *I Claudius* by Robert Graves, also *The Unlikely Pilgrimage of Fry* by Rachael Joyce. *Stoner* by John Edward Williams.

Claire Ighodara, Lloyds of London: *Long Walk to Freedom*, Nelson Mandela.

Cornelia Meyer, Gasol: *The Divine Comedy* by 13th century Italian writer Dante Alighieri.

Davida Marston, Bank of Ireland: *Life After Life* by Kate Atkinson, *Citizen Quinn* by Ian Kehoe and Gavin Daly, *Enron: The Smartest Guys in the Room* by S Boswell, *Fool's Gold* by Gillian Tett, *Organising Genius* by Warren G. Bennis

Fiona Cannon, Lloyds Banking Group: Hillary Clinton's *Hard Choices*.

Fleur Bothwick, EY: *Quiet* by Susan Cain, *30 Lies About Money* by Peter Koenig.

Heather Rabbatts, The Football Association: James Joyce *Ulysses*.

Jo Valentine, London First: *The Snow Geese* by William Fiennes.

Judith Mayhew Jonas, London & Partners: *Daughter of the Forest* by Juliet Marillier.

Kate Blackett, MediaCom: *The Pirate Inside* by Adam Morgan, *Tell The Truth* by Sue Unerman.

Kate Robertson, Havas Worldwide: *The Lie*. Helen Dunmore.

Kirsten English, eFront: *How to Build a Habitable Planet* by Charles H. Langmuir and Wally Broecker.

Melanie Richards, KPMG: *The Value of Difference* by Binna Kandola.

Natalie Griffiths, DWF: *The Kite Runner*, Khalid Hosseini.

Paula Vennells, The Post Office: *Leading at the Edge: Leadership Lessons from the Extraordinary Saga of Shackleton's Antarctic Expedition*

by Dennis N. T. Perkins, Margaret P. Holtman, Paul R. Kessler, Catherine Mccarthy.

Patience Wheatcroft, FIAT: *Long Walk To Freedom*, Nelson Mandela.

Sharon Thorne, Deloitte: *The Chimp Paradox* by Dr Steve Peters.

Sheekha Rajani: Diversity Jobs: *The Girl Who Kicked the Hornet's Nest* by Stieg Larsson.

Toni Belcher: *The Hare with Amber Eyes* by Edmund de Waal.

Trusha Kachhela, PwC: *The Little Coffee Shop of Kabul* by Deborah Rodriguez.

7 TOP RESPONSES ON LEADERSHIP
MISTAKES YOU MUST AVOID

1   **Andrea Wong, Sony Pictures Entertainment:** Not making decisions. Don't fear making decisions, you are holding the business back if you think you are not part of the decision making. You will make mistakes, but it's OK.

2   **Judith Mayhew Jonas, London & Partners:** The biggest mistake leaders make, and this is often when they've been in power for a very long time, is they begin to believe their own rhetoric and their own propaganda and they can't be challenged because people are too frightened to tell them the reality. The emperor has no clothes.

3   **Kirsten English, eFront:** The essence of good business is being in touch with your customers. Some leaders lose sight of the reason they are there. So they forgot to be real.

4   **Melanie Richards, KPMG:** Communication. People know when leaders are not being authentic, when they don't believe what they are saying or do not have a strong sense of direction or purpose. The leaders, if they can't convey authenticity – it's a real challenge.

EDUCATION

5 **Sharon Thorne, Deloitte:** Lots of leaders are guilty of failing to listen. Mostly from time pressure, they don't really listen to what people are saying and are not reading the mood music around the board.

6 **Sheekha Rajani, Diversity Jobs:** Sometimes when you come up the ladder it can be very easy to get caught up in the details. You have people there you can rely on, you are there to lead and inspire, don't get caught up in detail as it is not your place. Have faith in your team.

7 **Trusha Kachhela, PwC:** From a male's perspective, they tend to be afraid to ask females what they perceive as difficult questions such as what are their aspirations, especially those who have just come back from maternity leave. They feel they can't ask them about what they want to achieve in their careers. This is a huge mistake, particularly when you have women who don't say and men who don't ask – what will you get? Nothing!

7 TOP MASTERCLASS
OF LIFE RESPONSES

❖ Your determination to make it to the top and stay there – you only get one chance so make it count.

❖ Anyone can succeed no matter their background.

❖ Self-belief – you have to believe in yourself or no one else will believe in you.

❖ Family comes first.

❖ Collaboration – essential to work with and take other people with you.

❖ Networking – keeping talking to people, communication is key.

❖ Resilience – understand life is the long game.

7 TOP WAYS OF LIFELONG LEARNING RESPONSES

1 **Beatriz Araujo, Baker & McKenzie:** Keep looking for challenges, but always reflect to see what you've achieved or what you might have done better.

2 **Davida Marston, Bank of Ireland:** CPD (Continuous Professional Development) is absolutely essential.

3 **Fiona Cannon:** Watching and learning from people doing great things and talking to them.

4 **Fleur Bothwick, EY:** Continue to network a lot and make new opportunities work for you.

5 **Jo Valentine, London First:** Learn new languages, take new courses, it stretches the mind and I think a little humility is important. So knowing that you never reach nirvana, and knowing that you have more to learn is an education in itself. The first time I spoke at the House of Lords Chamber was a huge learning opportunity.

6 **Natalie Griffiths, DWF:** Take yourself out of your comfort zone. I will on an annual basis do something that takes me out of my personal comfort zone. That's strengthening my tool kit.

7 **Sharon Thorne, Deloitte:** I do have a coach, not a friend, not family, and not someone who I work with. She has a very high level of EQ (Emotional Intelligence) and being able to talk with someone like that and ask difficult questions forces me to look inward and helps me to develop the self-awareness I need to be a better leader. I have been with Deloitte for 27 years and never feel that I have stood still. I'm always being given something new or asking for something new that keeps me developing.

EDUCATION

EDUCATION NOTES PAGE

List 7 things you have learned and can implement on **Education**:

1 _____

_____

_____

2 _____

_____

_____

3 _____

_____

_____

4 _____

_____

_____

5 _____

_____

_____

6 _____

_____

_____

7 _____

_____

_____

LEADERS

ADVICE

"To accept good advice is but to increase one's own ability."

Johann Wolfgang Von Goethe

ADVICE

Accepting advice and information is an art; power comes with how you use it!

THERE TENDS to be a misconception that asking for advice or mentoring is somehow weak or unprofessional. As women, we wish to appear competent at all times when operating within a corporate environment. However, competence stems from the ability to utilise all resources, including examining the journey of those who have already travelled the corporate path successfully.

For this reason, the importance of peer review, mentoring and advice from senior co-workers cannot be emphasised enough as playing a pivotal role in career advancement.

Those who have been fortunate enough to work with talented and experienced individuals should have capitalised on their colleagues' ability to guide them in the right direction and share their knowledge, wisdom and experiences. But as Publilius Syrus once stated, "Many receive advice, few profit by it."

So many people are resistant to accepting advice that they miss out on a wealth of input for boosting their career.

Women seem to be credited with listening and accepting advice more than their male counterparts, although this is a generalisation which surely cannot apply to all. There is, however, no denying that male or female, one needs continuous professional growth in order to contribute successfully to the corporate environment. One of the best ways to achieve this is to study those who have already achieved the desired results. What better way to learn how to re-enact the successful strategies of others than to ask them how they did it?

It's clear that some people will not wish to share their success secrets with you, but it might be a surprising revelation how many people are more than happy to impart their advice in relation to climbing the corporate ladder. It might have something to do with Joseph Joubert's adage, "To teach is to learn twice over". In the exchange of advice, both the giver and receiver benefit: the receiver learns something new and the giver's knowledge and confidence is reinforced. The interviewees in this book all took valuable time out of their incredibly busy schedules to contribute to your success by sharing their experiences and advice on how to climb successfully to the corporate board as a female individual. It's a testament to their professionalism that they don't covet their expertise but want to share it with others wishing to emulate their successes.

There is however a caveat to taking advice and emulating the actions of others which is to give credit where credit is due. If you have been inspired by or developed in some way through the knowledge, experience and advice of someone else, feel free to say so and/or pass on what you have learned. Taking credit for ideas or actions which did not originate with you can at best make you seem less trustworthy should anybody discover that they are not your ideas. In the worst case scenario, what you are doing could actually be viewed as plagiarism and lead to a serious dent in your reputation or even legal complications.

You'll note that many women in this book attribute elements of their success to named mentors, advisors and role models, and this is part of the cycle of success. Others contribute to your success and should therefore be acknowledged. In return you should contribute to the success of those around you and also be acknowledged for doing so. Through these mutual endorsements, a network of trust and cooperation will be built around you, strengthening your chances of climbing the corporate ladder in a sustainable and positive way.

Now here is your chance to benefit from the wealth of advice given by some of the top female board members in the UK.

The women I have chosen under this particular section stood out for me for giving exemplar career advice.

ADVICE

MELANIE RICHARDS
VICE CHAIR KPMG

MELANIE RICHARDS

Melanie Richards is Vice Chair of KPMG UK, providing high quality advice on a global scale. She is also a partner at KPMG in Capital Advisory Services. Melanie advises clients on financings of up to several billion pounds. Since joining the firm, Melanie, who has successfully developed the Debt Advisory Practice, is a strong supporter of gender diversity through company-wide initiatives. She is co-chair of the Women's Network and plays an active role in mentoring and coaching. Additionally Melanie hosts Senior Business Women's Network events to support promoting women up the corporate ladder. Before joining KPMG to set up the practice, she spent 18 years in banking, 15 of which at NatWest doing a variety of roles including working on the trading floor, originating bonds and private placements and working with credit committees. She subsequently moved on to Hambros to head up their private placement group. So she has had quite a broad and varied career. She didn't actually start out with any plan... for example you can't schedule when you have children, but she is married and has two wonderful boys. She is also on the board of the Eve Appeal Charity which funds research into gynaecological cancers and Orbis UK which is a sight-saving charity. She is on the board of governors at Eastbourne College and on the steering committee of the 30% Club. Although Melanie is in the business of giving advice on an extensive scale, it is her commitment to other women through her capacity to give advice, support, mentor and coach that places her strongly in this category within the L.E.A.D.E.R.S. traits. Throughout my journey speaking to women on boards, I heard a constant observation from the women that women aren't as good at helping other women up the ladder as their male counterparts. Melanie is quite obviously the exception to that alleged rule. Whilst this might have had something to do with the scarcity of women on boards, it's not a stretch to consider that once women make it into the boardroom, they feel they have to work twice as hard to stay in

ADVICE

the boardroom, thus having little time to share themselves around. If it is to be accepted that women on boards find it difficult to help other women, then Melanie Richards smashes that perception wide open. Melanie is well regarded for her tireless contributions to the gender conversation through the networks she contributes to and the numerous mentoring and coaching commitments she maintains with the intention to share her skills and to keep the door to the top room open. Being the visible trailblazer she is for other women to emulate, I had a few questions about advice for her to answer.

BEST ADVICE EVER GIVEN:

Melanie's response was focused: "In the mad world of 24/7, it's important to never forget the part you play in this world or in business… most importantly never lose sight of who you are."

ADVICE TO WOMEN ASPIRING TO THE BOARDROOM:

"Motivation is quite simple, only do things you care about. If you don't care about it, you cannot be motivated." Melanie went on to say, "I've been very fortunate – I've enjoyed everything that I do and that's what keeps me motivated. When you are looking at opportunities, think about it from the perspective of what you care about, what will surprise and challenge you. From an aspirational perspective, it's about making the best of opportunities that come your way. Networking is good. I'm a bit of convert to the formalised networking, though most of the power is in informal networking and how you follow up and use the contacts around you without being annoying to people." That was a very relevant point. There were times when I am more concerned about the balance between being a pest and being an effective networker. I was very reassured that Melanie had considered that too. Melanie continued, "Think about that map of who are the people that are going to want to help you, as opposed to those who you think should be helping you, and about how you can help them, as there needs to be mutual interest and reciprocity. With respect to preservation, it is important to recognise balance," Melanie continued. "I don't have an unrealistic perspective of work-life balance. You shouldn't call it work-life balance — it should be work-life fit as this is a far better way of expressing it. Sometimes work has to take priority and sometimes friends and family have to take priority, but it is important to work out what that balance is."

ADVICE FOR FUTURE LEADERS:

"Being good at maths, feeling comfortable around numbers is a practical point. Do not underestimate that. Whilst it won't take you all the way, energy and enthusiasm and really going for what you want is a big factor in getting to the top. Most of the people around me that I regard as very successful got there because they grabbed opportunities each time they presented themselves. If you sit back waiting for it to happen to you, it very rarely does. But if you are there looking for opportunities, radiating enthusiasm and delivering then I think they will come to you."

ADVICE

BARONESS JO VALENTINE
CEO LONDON FIRST

BARONESS JO VALENTINE

Baroness Josephine Valentine is a member of the House of Lords and CEO of London First. She joined the London First profit organisation in 1997 as managing director. Jo previously worked at Barings Bank where she was the first female manager; she was also one of the first female managers at the BOC Group. In her time Jo has started many organisations and the Blackburn Partnership, a regeneration company, was one of her first, with a remit to help regeneration across Lancashire. She is also a member of Peabody Trust and a fellow of St Hugh's College, Oxford.

Jo is the CEO of London First, a business campaign group focused on making London the best city in the world in which to do business. It is a members body of senior business people working together to do what they can to make London a city others want to come to do business in and run their business. She is also on the board of Peabody Trust which has a billion pounds worth of social housing in London, so Jo has a lot of responsibility. In her London First capacity she has been on various boards. "We often create other organisations of which I am on the board and then spin them off. Anything from Teach First which we created ten years ago, to something called Skills Company, of which I'm on the board, which holds the largest careers and jobs fairs in London with over 30,000 job opportunities for young people."

Jo Valentine is the epitome of a person with diversity embedded in her work life. She is recognised as a free thinker with an open mind. Being on the board of Peabody Trust and other community organisations, her experience with race and gender issues gives her the edge on diversity that is necessary to survive in one of the most diverse working cities in the world. I wanted to hear her views on diversity in the work place, especially from a gender point of view. Here's how she answered my questions:-

ADVICE

BEST ADVICE EVER GIVEN:

"My husband taught me about diplomacy when I was younger, when I was like a bull in a china shop. He taught me about saying things the way other people want to see it, as opposed to the way I would see it. Also presenting an agreement to your advantage rather than what I want."

ADVICE TO WOMEN ASPIRING TO THE BOARDROOM:

"Hold your nerve and stick to what you believe to be right. A lot of people coming out of exec to board will find it very tough to find the right board – that's about networking and keeping in the loop. Find the right people and surround yourself with them."

ADVICE TO FUTURE LEADERS:

"Depends on what they want to go into. Whatever it is, suppose life is constant learning. Eleanor Roosevelt said life is constant learning. One step at a time, try various things, don't be disappointed if you fail, once, twice, get up and make the change needed to move on, try to work through what works for you. Experience counts so try lots of things."

KAREN BLACKETT OBE
CEO MEDIACOM

KAREN BLACKETT OBE

Our third woman on a board to feature in the advice section is none other than Karen Blackett OBE.

Karen has been in media for 20 years and, as the Chief Executive Officer, she leads the largest media agency in the UK, MediaCom. As the CEO, Karen controls over £1.2bn of media billings, leading over 900 people, and in 2013 led the agency to win over £160m of new business, not bad for someone who left university with a degree in geography. "I wasn't sure what I wanted to do," Karen recounted. She originally applied for a job on The Independent as a media researcher that would eventually set her on her way. "During the interview they decided that my skill set was better placed in negotiating media space, which was to become my first real step in getting where I am today." Her Barbadian parents were a little apprehensive at first. "At the time they were expecting me to be a doctor, lawyer, teacher or an accountant. So when I told them I was a media buyer, they had no idea what that was, and didn't know anyone else that did that, so it was new ground for all of them."

Well, Karen's determination has paid off on a grand scale. In recent years Karen has been personally recognised in the media industry for her contributions. Karen featured twice in 'Management Today's "35 Under 35" article and five times in the Power List of the UK's 100 most influential black people, most recently in 2014, where she came in at number 5. In 2013 Karen received a special award at the Women In Marketing Awards. Karen received an OBE in the Queen's 2014 Birthday Honours List. She is also a trustee of charity 'Adopt a Better Way' and was a finalist in the Veuve Clicquot Business Women Awards 2014.

Karen continued, "I loved my new adventure, I've always loved communicating, I love people and I love finding out about people and why they would choose one particular brand over another, and about being able to build empathy from one brand to a consumer."

Karen worked her way up the media industry ladder, as she moved around agencies. She had key roles where she was responsible for new business and marketing. "This made you ensure that you were accountable, as it is the lifeblood of any agency," she recalled.

Karen also moved around where she became responsible for Europe and Africa which was a massive learning curve for her as it taught her about different cultures and how to lead them. It also taught her a lot about bringing people on side, about various employment laws and how they are applied in different countries. Karen spent a lot of time in Moscow, Turkey, Warsaw, Spain and France, after which she came back to the UK. It was at this time Karen had her proudest moment in life, the birth of her son Isaac.

Yet Karen's position in the advice section of the L.E.A.D.E.R.S. traits for women on boards isn't just because she is the head of the largest media buying company in the UK, advising others where and when to spend their budgets for the best return on investment, it is because of the important spear-heading work she is doing with young people who want to find a route into the media industry. In 2012 Karen launched the first media buying agency apprentice scheme encouraging young people from all backgrounds to get a foothold in the industry.

BEST ADVICE EVER GIVEN:

"Two ears, one mouth, use them in that order. So listen before you open your mouth, and make an impact. I see a number of male leaders speak without hearing, so they make basic decisions without an insight.

Also have a team of peer leaders, having people you can bounce off outside the agency with issues you are facing, debating, challenging. Having a range of people to ratify what you feel instinctively is great."

ADVICE

ADVICE TO WOMEN ASPIRING TO THE BOARDROOM:

"Having cheerleaders is really important, and that would come from having a range of people that you can go to. The networking element is so important. In this role as CEO I have been exposed to so many people, and making those opportunities count is important. I have learnt in a room to make sure that I don't get stuck in one conversation no matter how fascinating and interesting and that I do talk to other people. Just do your job really well. Don't focus on the next role or position because you get that next role or position by focusing on what you do incredibly well; you get noticed. So many people are worried about the next step that they don't put 120% into the one they are currently doing. There is no time limit or right time, focus on the here and now."

ADVICE TO FUTURE LEADERS:

"Make sure that you are really good at maths. It's so true in business. Understanding a balance sheet and a P&L. No matter what you end up doing, reading the business accounts is really important, as are many different areas of business. Try to get exposure to as many areas of the business as you can. Whether it is manufacturing, engineering, communications, technology, just to get a sense of what is going on in the business world."

LEADERS

KIRSTEN ENGLISH
NED EFRONT

KIRSTEN ENGLISH

For some of the women on boards that I interviewed, being able to steer a company here in the UK is the pinnacle of their achievements. However, what do you say about a woman who has been effective here and in Europe? Kirsten English, a cool, stylish and effervescent business woman, is just such a person. Kirsten has held down Non-Executive and Executive roles for public companies listed in London, Dublin, NASDAQ and Oslo Non-Executive. She is currently a Non-Executive Director of eFront, Contis and Birdstep, a Norwegian company, one of which is not only a private equity, but has a minority quota for the board which means the boards are balanced in the numbers of men and women. Kirsten responds, "I went on the boards here before the quota system happened, but it is quite unique as there is always a gender balance on the board." There is a commonality on all three boards that Kirsten currently sits on. They have private equity backing with small numbers of shareholders, rather than public boards where there are many shareholders. Moreover they are all in the technology domain.

Kirsten started in Reuters, now Thomson Reuters. Kirsten explains, "The advantage to that is when you join a large company you get a lot of generalist experience about how companies operate and you get some perception of different types of people and cultures in the same company. You also get the idea of geographic diversity and how perhaps to speak and work with people who don't have English as their first language or were brought up with a different working style". She goes on, "I can't recommend starting in a large company enough to get that experience, get a Rolodex going, and from the start of your career perhaps in another area which perhaps is a jump from that experience. You have to think about what you can contribute, what's your speciality, are you interested in business?"

Kirsten had something to say about Sweden too. "In Sweden there is still quite a lot of competition to get on boards, but it is a great place to go and do business, as they do have a very different style, and a great diversity of businesses there. In the tech world there's a lot of things starting up there and being exported around the world. It's also an early adopter of technology ideas and cultures, and the modern generation is very much into social media."

Kirsten lives in London, but has lived in several places around the world. She explains, "The longest I've lived anywhere is Sweden."

Kirsten has a positive view on Norway: "In many respects Norway is a geographical area which is a bit ahead in its thinking, but it is culturally appropriate to a country where people's executive careers in terms of men and women and the workplace also reflect gender diversity positively."

With all her international experience and more so in Sweden and Norway, the places where diversity on boards is part of the fabric, in addition to the fact that the technology sector is a tough industry for women, I felt Kirsten is best placed to be within the advice section of the L.E.A.D.E.R.S. Kirsten is able to give that international perspective from one of the toughest industry sectors for women, and also, given her experience in territories where quotas are in place, as well as in the UK where quotas are not accepted, I thought she could give a unique view of both sides of that coin.

BEST ADVICE EVER GIVEN:

"Run a business for cash, not for profit. Profit is vanity, cash is reality. I think definitely if you are in a smaller environment, focus on cash as you will see how that pays people's wages."

ADVICE TO WOMEN ASPIRING TO THE BOARDROOM:

"Question your motivation for going on a board. Some people just want to be on a board, and that's not necessarily the right way to think about a board. You have to know what you will contribute

ADVICE

to this board. It's either a speciality, it could be legal, accounting or communication, or you are an industry-knowledgeable person.

By showing sound judgment, maturity and experience in relation to an executive career and perhaps through a couple of industries really equips you to be there."

ADVICE TO FUTURE LEADERS:

"You need basic skills if you are going into the business world. Focus on maths, economics, read the papers, understand what is going on in the industry you are interested in. Have a very credible email address, always be polite in your correspondence and spell things correctly. Manage your social media presence with care. Speak to people. Arrive on time and be courteous. Look for internships. Two thirds of graduate jobs are achieved as a result of having had some work experience. Also ladies, take inspiration from JK Rowling who said, 'If you want to be a world-beating authoress, you don't do the housework and you don't iron anybody else's shirts.'"

OVERVIEWS: ADVICE

BEST ADVICE EVER GIVEN:

With a range of advice on offer, this is probably the most informative gathering of information in one place you will ever get from women on boards, from very personal perspectives of the best advice ever given to inspire and motivate women aspiring to the boardroom.

Andrea Wong: Use the words 'yes' and 'thank you' as much as you can, you'd be surprised how far politeness and charm can get you.

Carole Stone: Don't put things off. It's as easy to do it today as tomorrow.

Claire Ighodaro: Your success is not defined by the failure of others and it is not decided by the failure of others. Competition is important but it's not about others failing –it's about you doing your very best.

Davida Marston: Well, believe in yourself funnily enough, because it's not a given. Most of us have great self-doubts and so I think to have belief, to be determined and not to take no for an answer is essential. Be aware that men and women communicate differently, that's a very important piece of advice.

Heather Rabbatts: The best piece of advice I was given when things go wrong, and they always do, is to understand not to lose your head. What do you take out of a crisis to find an opportunity? That was probably the best advice.

Fleur Bothwick: If in doubt, ask.

Jo Valentine: My husband taught me about diplomacy when I was younger. I was like a bull in a china shop. He taught me about saying things the way other people want to hear it, as opposed to the way I would see it. Also presenting an agreement to your advantage rather than what I want.

Judith Mayhew Jonas: The best piece of advice I was ever given was, seize every opportunity and make the most of it.

Kate Robertson: I was told at 33 I was not very impressive as at that time I did not know what I wanted to do, and I should take a breath, sit down, and think about my career before I went any further. The way in which it was said gave me such a shock. It made me stop and think. It was very good advice.

Melanie Richards: It's easy to live in the mad world of 24/7, but it's important to never forget who you are.

Natalie Griffin: Not to be so hard on myself. You've achieved 80% of what you are really good at and other people recognise it. The 20% is your learning curve – use it well and get better. You will never get a 100% first time. Use the 20% to gauge yourself going forward.

Paula Vennells: Respect your time, and it's been the best piece of advice ever. You'll never get it back.

Patience Wheatcroft: Ask the simple questions and keep asking until you are satisfied with the answers given.

Sharon Thorne: It was ruthless prioritising because I like to get involved and say yes to lots of people. My coach pointed out that the way I've always solved things is to throw time at it, now I've run out of time, so prioritise.

Sheekha Rajani: Ensure you understand what your career values and drivers are and really go back to the self-awareness piece. If you are true to your values and your drivers, and find, organise and align to them, you will be able to propel yourself in whatever you set yourself up to do next.

Toni Belcher: Never prejudge, assume or presume anything.

Trusha Kachhela: I had a wobble on my transition to partner. I was nervous before deciding how to move forward and was told to be comfortable in my own skin. If I was never given that chance or that advice I would not be here now. It gave me the confidence to move on. It's very personal to me and I'm not sure how it would apply to someone else. Visualising yourself in the position you want to be in is a good way of achieving that comfort ability.

TO WOMEN ASPIRING TO THE BOARDROOM:

M.A.P your way to the boardroom: What is your motivation for being on a board? How will you get there? Once you are there, how will you stay there? Here our women give advice on Motivation, Aspirations and Preservation, on getting to and staying in the boardroom.

Andrea Wong: Motivation: If you are motivated to be on a board, networking and letting people know is the best way to start getting there. **Aspiration:** Choose a board where you can really add to it and you will grow from it and also bring a different perspective. **Preservation:** My boards make me better at my job, as they help me to bring a different perspective, and will help me last in that position longer.

LEADERS

Beatriz Araujo: Motivation is key. I personally need to get up every day feeling excited about what I am about to do. Not that every day is a great day, but you look forward to the day and want to achieve something that day. Find something you want to do. Otherwise the motivation goes, performance goes. **Aspiration**: You have to look at different stages during your career, it's always healthy to look ahead, but be present in your job. **Preservation**: Keep focused on what you want to achieve, be true to yourself and keep in touch with reality, family, hobbies. Life is more than just your job.

Claire Ighodaro: Motivation: you have to be very motivated. It is hard work and you are taking on a great deal of responsibility. You are taking on personal reputational risk and you are expected, once you are on that board, to commit, so you have to be motivated. **Aspiration**: If you don't have the aspiration there is no point in you trying. Perhaps you should question why you want to be on a board. **Preservation**: Resilience is important. If you do the work required of you, if you keep up with the board, if you keep up with your continuous professional development, keep up with your learning, then that should help you on the preservation front.

Cornelia Meyer: Motivation: I think what women need to do is they need something to work towards; they need to know they want to get on boards. They need to start networking. **Aspiration:** I will tell women not to be too overt and too aggressive because again, if you go out there and say, I have a friend who has been, and done that, to everybody, I want to be on the board, I want to be on the board, it will probably not happen. **Preservation:** When you get there ensure you keep selling yourself in a professional way.

Davida Marston: Well actually, this is one of the hardest ones to answer because I think it very much depends on the woman and it depends on the organisation. I don't actually think these are gender specific. I think the type of organisation you are joining will determine it to some degree. Manage how you need to behave in that environment, but I think you do need to have an aspiration. I

ADVICE

think it helps to have a plan. I think it helps to be very clear about it. If you are young, you probably haven't had a chance to develop the USP (unique selling proposition), but as we get older, we need to be very clear about the ways in which we add value. Now, that doesn't necessarily mean work specific, it could be in a style, or a behaviour, but we do need to be very clear that we are there to deliver value and we need to be able to quantify that, I think.

Fiona Cannon: First of all, be really clear about why you want to be on a board, because I think the thing for me was, and it's also typical of the kinds of boards I've been involved in, when I was secretary chair of the commission there, I was thinking this is going to be fantastic. We're going to be thinking about big strategic things, having big important conversations about how to make things different, and of course you do but actually a lot of it's about governance. It's about all the quite mundane things. So you have to really think about why you want to be involved. And be really clear why you're doing it. Because you'll need that, at those points where you start to think, why am I having this conversation about these kinds of things. So I think that's the first thing.

The second thing I think is really about building your allies on the board as well. So in terms of 'if you get onto a board' before your first board meeting, try to meet as many people as possible beforehand. Again that sounds very straight-forward advice but actually it's really important, I think, to feel when you're first meeting, that someone's there and looking out for you. And it's important as it goes forward that you understand that you've got some support and you build that support amongst your colleagues on the board. And so those, I think, are really important pieces of advice, the things that were very important to me when I first started out. And in terms of the aspiration aspect, I think that's for me about aspiration for the organisation you're involved in. So it goes back to this whole thing about choosing, why you're going to the place, you're on that board that you're thinking of going on, be it a company or whatever it is. What are your aspirations for the company as well? So that you can be part of building something broader than just about your own aspirations.

Preservation I think comes from that whole element about building your allies and so making sure that you've got that backing. I think sometimes what happens is that you can get too tied up in the task. So in terms of delivery and being really focused on delivery, that sometimes means that the other bits that go round leadership fall away. Be that about coaching or developing or the other thing that's very important clearly. All leaders need to have a vision of the future and think strategically, but not making the time to have those strategic thoughts and thinking about where you want to go can be detrimental. Because you're too present in the 'today', this can sometimes be a problem.

Fleur Bothwick: The sooner you start thinking about your career the better. Start early, start small and build on experience.

Heather Rabbatts: In terms of advice for women in the boardroom, "Is that where I want to be?" You don't just go there because you think you should or because it ticks the CV box. It's because you think that that's an area that you want to be involved in. So the motivational point is, first of all understand whether it's somewhere that you want to be and that also gives you an opportunity to be with other people from different walks of life who you will also be able to share different experiences with. That also links to the preservation point that being with people who are very good at what they do helps to preserve you, protect you, because these are challenging roles, you have many duties and responsibilities. People can fall foul of different company codes so you want to feel that you limit your exposure by sitting alongside people who are very capable. Also in terms of preservation, as a woman I think being able to meet other women, non-execs, and share experiences so that you can feel less alone, because often we all are in those boardrooms pretty much by ourselves.

ADVICE

157

Jo Valentine: Motivation: Find the right people and surround yourself with them. **Aspiration:** A lot of people coming out of exec to board will find the right board very tough to find, so that's about networking and keeping in the loop. **Preservation:** Hold your nerve and stick to what you believe to be right.

Karen Blackett: Motivation: Having cheerleaders is really important, and that would come from having a range of people that you can go to. The networking element is so important. In this role as CEO I have been exposed to so many people, and making those opportunities count is important. I have learnt in a room to make sure that I don't get stuck in one conversation no matter how fascinating and interesting and that I do talk to other people. **Aspiration:** Just do your job really well. Don't focus on the next role or position because you get that next role or position by focusing on what you do incredibly well – you get noticed. **Preservation:** So many people are worried about the next step that they don't put 120% into the one they are currently doing. There is no time limit or right time, focus on the here and now.

Kate Robertson: Motivation: You have to have a goal – decide what you want and commit yourself to it. To keep you motivated, tell others that's what you want to do, and what you expect. You have to accept that you may fail and feel temporarily humiliated thereby. It's very motivating to open up to and having to commit to something, then go and get it; rather than not telling anyone and then if it fails saying, well I did not want it anyway. **Aspiration:** At that level where you might aspire to be on the board, if you don't have the aspiration no-one will have it for you. You should, if you've got that far, go for board. It's a very influential position and you can change the course and culture of organisations and make a difference. It is vital to commit to 'that's what I'm here to do', to be the best and be on the board, be present. If you don't, you won't. **Preservation:** It is so tough for women. Assuming you've got on to a board you will need allies, you might think you won't but you will. It will be political, not personal. Whether you are young or old, beautiful or ugly, there's always someone out to get you. I don't know why. Sometimes that's just how it is. Because women are so few on boards or on their board they will find themselves with no allies. So even if you get to the board you will still have to keep proving yourself even more than any man in the same position. So you will definitely need allies and we don't have allies when we get to that position. It's not honest or objective, and I think that in there is one of the elements of what holds women back as well.

Kirsten English: Motivation: Question your motivation for going on a board. Some people just want to be on a board, and that's not necessarily the right way to think about a board. **Aspiration:** You have to know what you will contribute to this board. It's either a speciality, it could be legal, accounting or communication, or you are an industry-knowledgeable person. **Preservation:** Showing sound judgment, maturity and experience probably in an executive career and perhaps through a couple of industries really equips you to be there.

Melanie Richards: Motivation is quite simple, only do thing you care about; if you don't care, you cannot be motivated. I've been very fortunate I've enjoyed everything that I do and I think that's what keeps me motivated. When you are looking at opportunities think about it from the perspective of what you care about, what will surprise and challenge you. **Aspiration:** make the best of opportunities that come your way. Networking is good, I'm a convert to formalised networking though most of the power is in informal networking and how you follow up and use the contacts around you without being annoying to people. Think about that M.A.P. – who are the people that are going to want to help you, as opposed to those who you think should be helping you, and about how you can help them as there needs to be mutual interest and reciprocity. **Preservation:** It is important to recognise balance. I don't have an unrealistic perspective of work-life balance. You shouldn't call it work-life balance, it should

ADVICE

be work-life fit, a far better way of expressing it. Sometimes work has to take priority and sometimes friends and family have to take priority but it is important to work out what that balance is.

Natalie Griffin: Motivation: Try to do something you enjoy, as the more you enjoy something the better you are at it and the more you'll be able to rise through the ranks. Don't feel you have to tick every single box when going for the promotion, but ensure it's what you want. **Aspiration**: There shouldn't be a glass ceiling. I know that some people encounter it and feel that they have to work differently. You have to approach the workplace in terms of, 'it doesn't exist'. Emotionally, if you are trying to break through something, it's very difficult because if you are constantly trying to modify yourself, what of yourself is left. **Preservation**: Be accountable, make sure that when you say you are going to do something that you do it. Make sure people know that you are reliable and when say you are going to deliver – deliver. Take accountability and ownership. Because then they will always pick the best person for the job and hopefully that will be you. Never, never cry in the office!

Paula Vennells: Motivation: In terms of motivation, the advice is that you can be on that board, there's no reason why not. It's a confidence issue; perhaps we don't think about how far we can push ourselves. Again it comes back to the same thing – you can actually, you absolutely can. Prepare before a board meeting. Not just reading through the board papers but thinking about where different board colleagues are going to be coming from, trying to second guess the questions that might come up, listening, taking account of the advice of these people around the table and also being prepared to say you got things wrong. If you got things wrong, you're human just like everybody else. The last thing I would say is to remember that everybody else is human as well and that you're part of the same team.

Patience Wheatcroft: Motivation: You have to really want to do this. Accept that there are frustrations with being a non-exec.

Be prepared for a process that takes time. **Aspiration:** Aspire to dizzying heights – if you put limits on your aspiration you will be limited. **Preservation:** If you are nervous about preserving yourself, your role or any other aspect of life, then you probably won't take up challenges. It comes back to the authenticity point. It is important to be yourself and believe that you are comfortable and confident in presenting your views at boardroom tables. There will be people there who will be allies and you should build relationships.

Sharon Thorne: Motivation: Being on boards is a great experience, you can get a lot out of it. I think lots more women should try to do this. Loads of women have the capability and skills – they just have to believe in themselves. **Aspiration:** You have to be realistic to begin with. If you've never been on a board, it's unlikely you will go straight onto a FTSE100 but there are lots of boards for you start with. Set your sights high because women have the capability to be on boards.

Sheekha Rajani: Motivation: Build on your career values and drivers, understanding your motivation. Women can put a lot of pressure on themselves to be perfect and to be star students when growing up. It's OK not to be perfect, follow your own path, don't compete, differentiate if you see your peers perhaps taking the same path and being a bit quicker. Don't worry – things will come to you when it's right for you. **Aspiration:** Don't say no. Women are pragmatic and practical so when opportunities are presented, they think about the delivery before saying yes. Say yes, then worry about it later. **Preservation:** Take a leap of faith as you'll find you are able to do things that you never knew you could.

Toni Belcher: Everyone I know pretty much has seen the challenge of women on boards and wants to be a part of the challenge. Obviously there's a big push to bring more females onto boards, to use their people skills and the way they implement their skills and the way they carry them out. Remember we talked about the softer side; I think the word soft is the wrong word but I think aspiration

– it would be great to see one day an all-woman board, and in a big organisation, even just to test it.

Trusha Kachhela: Motivation: If you know what you want to do, tell somebody. Males tell everyone what they want, females don't. We expect people to toughen us up and say 'actually, you are ready for a partner position – come with us'. Typically, if you are a man you knock doors down and let people know you are ready for partner, asking 'what do I need to do?' Women don't do that. **Aspiration:** Don't feel scared about telling someone what you want to do. If you want a position, let people know. They can't help you if they don't know. Don't limit your level. **Preservation:** As long as I am doing a good job and adding value, I will be here. When I stop doing that, I won't.

TO FUTURE LEADERS

Andrea Wong: Figure out what you are passionate about because you spend too many hours of your life working, so you should enjoy what you do. I really do believe that if you end up doing something you are passionate about, you will be better at it. Be fearless. I say a lot to people around me that if you're not failing, you're not trying hard enough. It's good to fail actually.

Beatriz Araujo: Women should talk to people who are in business. I think it's getting easier to get work placements and would definitely encourage them to see it first-hand. Read the business press to see what's going on.

Carole Stone: You should take interest in what's going on around you. You should go to as many debates as you can, join as many think-tanks as you can, read as much as you can, both newspapers and the business magazines.

Claire Ighodaro: Fundamentally you do need to study. You do need to get the best work experience you can. Tell your teachers what you

LEADERS

would like to do so that they can help you, and most important I think, find yourself some mentors.

Cornelia Meyer: I would advise women to be themselves. Take every opportunity you can get, every internship, every job opportunity. Take it and do the best you can. Build a reputation as a solid professional.

Davida Marston: Work hard, because the world doesn't owe you a living, and actually people value those who demonstrate true commitment.

Fiona Cannon: There is a lot of advice, lots of tips that I wish I'd been given when I was younger. First of all, be passionate about what you're doing. Find something that you really want to do, whatever it is, and have that passion because without it, it can actually be a bit of a slog. Get yourself a sponsor. Find someone that you admire, go and ask them for their advice and support. People love nothing more than being asked for their advice and support; it doesn't matter who they are. So don't be afraid to go and ask for it. Find out from people how they did it and what you can learn from them.

Network, really make sure that you get as many people in your corner as possible. This sounds a bit kind of motherhood and apple pie, but be nice to everyone. Also sometimes people make the mistake of thinking that it's only more senior people you have to be nice to. Actually it's about how you get things done and you've got to understand and recognise where power lies. It doesn't always lie with the most senior people in the room. So really understand where the power lies and who you need to get on side. Especially when you're starting out, people you're starting out with or you're coming across may well go on to do other things as well. Therefore, it's about making that impression as you go on. Those would be the first things that I would say to young people.

The best piece of advice I got very early on was 'don't take things personally'. When I first started in this field where nobody was really doing diversity, I'd have meetings where people would be shouting at me. I'd come back from meetings and I'd say, "I can't, my God, this is so awful" and "They don't like me" and "What have I done?". My then mentor Julie Mellor would say, "Look, it's not about you; they don't know you. They don't know who you are. They may have been having a bad day. It's about how they are. It's about them. It's not about you." Early on, actually, I think it was the most perfect piece of advice because it means that you're able to separate out what belongs to you; what belongs to someone else and this is very important.

Fleur Bothwick: I don't care about cronyism. Use your networks – use who you know to get work experience and/or apprenticeships.

Heather Rabbatts: The advice I'd offer is, if you want to be a future leader then it is about working hard, it is about learning, always trying to learn. Every opportunity you have, learn from both good leaders and bad leaders. One comes across leaders every day in one's life, whether it's in your office or your head teacher or seeing politicians or reading about business leaders. Try always to be looking for what you think, why is that person standing out? What's drawing your attention to them? So understanding all the time about the effectiveness of the different leaders who come into your life, but also looking for those opportunities. Sometimes volunteering in your work to do something additional because you will learn by doing that.

Jo Valentine: Depends on what women want to go into. I suppose life is constant learning. Eleanor Roosevelt said "life is constant learning". Take one step at a time, try various things, don't be disappointed if you fail, once or twice. Get up and make the changes needed to move on – try to work through what works for you. Experience counts for a lot, so try lots of things.

Judith Mayhew Jonas: I would say to any school leaver who had an interest in business, go for it. It is the most rewarding thing to do.

Kate Robertson: It is so humbling to look at these youngsters today. My only advice would be to ensure you have training and qualifications post school. If you are fortunate enough to have the opportunity to read law, accounting or medicine, go and get it and do it. You must choose carefully. There are also lots of evening and part time courses that will teach you – study.

Kirsten English: You need basic skills if you are going into the business world. Focus on maths, economics. Read the papers to understand what is going on in the industry you are interested in. Have a very credible email address, always be polite in your correspondence and spell things correctly. Manage your social media presence with care. Speak to people. Arrive on time and be courteous. Look for internships. Two thirds of graduate jobs are achieved as a result of having had some work experience.

Melanie Richards: Be good at and feel comfortable around maths is a practical point. Whilst it won't take you all the way, energy and enthusiasm and really going at things is a big factor. People around me who I regard as very successful is because they grabbed opportunities. If you sit back waiting for it to happen to you, it very rarely does. But if you are there looking for it and radiating enthusiasm then I think it will come to you.

Natalie Griffin: You have to believe in yourself. There will be people you meet along the way, leaders that you have that will inspire you and create confidence and give you certain elements of confidence. Don't look at the next person and think of all the reasons why they are better than you. You will always come across people who have better (or worse) experience, school results and homes. In the work environment, it's about a can-do attitude. People want people who can help them do their job better. Don't get stagnant.

Paula Vennells: I think it starts at a very simple level with education which is that you have to have maths and you have to have English because numbers and words are what we deal with. Then, above everything else, you have to have confidence and a desire to take opportunities as they come up and to recognise that you can enhance your career and other people's by working with other people. You can never ever do your job yourself and it's how you work with others that will make them and you successful. But you do actually have to have those basics of being able to read numbers and make sense of them and also, because we all have to do it at some stage, write reports and read them and very quickly be able to distil information in text.

Patience Wheatcroft: Before leaving school, get as much business knowledge and work experience you can. Running your own business is a great experience. Otherwise it's difficult for young people today to get going in business – the world is moving so fast that it's hard to get on that ladder. Try lots of different things to see what works for you. Not everyone can go to university so apprenticeships are great. Open University offers huge scope for study without running up a massive loan.

Sharon Thorne: Work out what you enjoy doing and what your strengths are. Then see if you can find something aligned to you. There are lots of routes you can go down… professional services, accountancy, law. You can do lots of different things, but work hard and you will succeed.

Sheekha Rajani: It's very competitive out there at the moment. Differentiate, don't compete. Have the self-awareness to know what your USP is. Know what your differentiator is and what will set you apart from others.

Toni Belcher: Never assume or presume.

Trusha Kachhela: Find something you really enjoy doing. Make work your passion then it becomes easy.

7 TOP PIECES OF BEST ADVICE
SHARED WITH ME

1 **Andrea Wong:** Use the words 'yes' and 'thank you' as much as you can.

2 **Claire Ighodaro:** Your success is not defined by the failure of others. Competition is important but it's not about others failing, it's about you doing your very best.

3 **Fleur Bothwick:** If in doubt, ask.

4 **Judith Mayhew Jonas:** The best piece of advice I was ever given was seize every opportunity and make the most of it.

5 **Melanie Richards:** It's easy to live in the mad world of 24/7, but it's important to never forget who you are.

6 **Natalie Griffin:** Not to be so hard on myself. You've achieved 80% you are really good at and other people recognise. The 20% is your learning curve – use it well and get better. You will never get 100% first time. Use the 20% to gauge yourself going forward.

7 **Sharon Thorne:** It was ruthless prioritising because I like to get involved and say yes to lots of people. My coach pointed out that the way I've always solved things is to throw time at it, now I've now run out of time so prioritise.

7 TOP PIECES OF M.A.P.
(MOTIVATION, ASPIRATION, PRESERVATION) ADVICE
FOR WOMEN WANTING TO BE ON BOARDS:

Here we have the tops tips from the M.A.P. trajectory to the top floor. These were the top tips I found that most resonate with me.

1 **Claire Ighodaro: Motivation:** You have to be very motivated. It is hard work, you are taking on a great deal of responsibility. **Aspiration:** If you don't have the aspiration there is no point you trying. **Preservation:** Resilience is a must.

ADVICE

2 **Karen Blackett: Motivation:** Build a support network around you. **Aspiration:** By focusing on what you do incredibly well – you will get noticed. **Preservation:** There is no time limit or right time, focus on the here and now.

3 **Kate Robertson: Motivation:** You have to accept that you may fail and feel temporarily humiliated thereby. **Aspiration:** It is vital to commit to your goal, to do, and to be, the best on the board. Be present. **Preservation:** It so tough for women. It will be political, not personal.

4 **Kirsten English: Motivation:** Question your motivation for going on a board. **Aspiration:** You have to know what you will contribute to this board or you won't be there for long. **Preservation:** Showing sound judgment, maturity and experience really equips you to be there.

5 **Melanie Richards: Motivation:** Simple, only do things you care about: if you don't care, you cannot be motivated. **Aspiration:** Make the best of opportunities that come your way. Networking is good. Formalised networking is the most powerful. **Preservation:** It is important to recognise balance. You shouldn't call it work-life balance, it should be work-life fit, a far better way of expressing it.

6 **Natalie Griffin: Motivation:** Don't feel you have to tick every single box when going for the promotion, but ensure it's what you want. **Aspiration:** There shouldn't be a glass ceiling. I know that some people encounter it and feel that they have to work differently. You have to approach workplace in terms of, 'it doesn't exist'. **Preservation:** Be accountable, make sure that when you say you are going to do something that you do it. Make sure people know that you are reliable, and when say you are going to deliver – deliver. Never, never cry in the office!

7 **Trusha Kachhela: Motivation:** If you know what you want to do, tell somebody. **Aspiration:** Don't limit your career level. **Preservation:** As long as you are doing a good job and adding value you will be here.

LEADERS

7 TOP TIPS FOR
FUTURE LEADERS:

Here are the 7 tips I found most interesting, and chose as my tops tips for future leaders. Remember they are purely arbitrary, some may or may not agree, but the fact is they are all open to interpretation, and are all available for you to decide.

1. **Andrea Wong:** Figure out what you are passionate about because you spend too many hours of your life working so you should enjoy what you do.

2. **Fleur Bothwick:** Don't worry about cronyism, use your networks, use who you know to get work experience and/or apprenticeships.

3. **Kate Robertson:** Ensure you have training and qualifications post school. Engage in lifelong learning.

4. **Kirsten English:** You need basic skills if you are going into the business world. Focus on maths, economics, read the papers, understand what is going on in the industry you are interested in. Have a very credible email address, always be polite in your correspondence and spell things correctly. Manage your social media presence with care. Speak to people. Arrive on time and be courteous. Look for internships. Two thirds of graduate jobs are achieved as a result of having had some work experience.

5. **Natalie Griffin:** You have to believe in yourself. There will be people you meet along with way, leaders that you have that will inspire you and create confidence and give you certain elements of confidence. Don't look at the next person and think of all the reasons why they are better than you. You will always come across people who have better experience, school results, homes. In the work environment it's about a can-do attitude. People want people who can help them do their job better. Don't get stagnant.

ADVICE

6   **Sheekha Rajani:** Differentiate, don't compete. Have the self-awareness to know what your differentiator is and what will set you apart from others.

7   **Trusha Kachhela:** Find something you really enjoy doing. Make work your passion then it becomes easy and you'll not get tired of it.

Did you find this useful? Why not email and tell me which of the tips you found most useful, and if you have your own, please email your tips to me, I will list them on the website and blog, and give you credit for doing so.

Website: **http://www.womenbusinessleaders.co.uk/contactus**

7 Traits Leadership Learning Limited
2 Tunstall Road, London SW9 8DA

Tel: **+44 (0)20 3086 9311**

Email: **7traits@7traits.co.uk**

Twitter: **@7traits**

LinkedIn Group: **7Traits**

Facebook Page: **7Traits**

Instagram: **7Traits**

Amazon: **http://www.bit.ly/seventraits**

ADVICE NOTES PAGE

List 7 things you have learned and can implement on **Advice**:

1 _____
_____
_____

2 _____
_____
_____

3 _____
_____
_____

4 _____
_____
_____

5 _____
_____
_____

6 _____
_____
_____

7 _____
_____
_____

ADVICE

DIVERSITY

*"Diversity: the art of thinking
independently together."*

Malcolm Stevenson Forbes

DIVERSITY

FORBES MAGAZINE recently reported on findings by Katherine Phillips, Associate Professor of Management and Organizations at Northwestern University Kellogg School of Management. In a study, homogeneous and diverse groups were compared in their task of trying to solve a murder mystery. Forbes reported that Phillips found the diverse groups felt that they didn't work together well or feel confident about decisions. This contrasted greatly with how the homogeneous groups felt. Interestingly enough though, Forbes found that the diverse groups consistently outperformed their homogeneous counterparts. The moral of this tale?

Dealing with diversity is far more challenging for the majority culture than avoidance of diversity issues. The benefits, however, far outweigh the luxury of remaining within the comfort zone of non-inclusion.

And what is more crucial to success than recognising what works best, despite appearances? There is almost no doubt that, across the board, diversity works. If for no other reason, the mere inclusion of different perspectives, opinions and backgrounds can have unquestionably positive knock-on effects:

1 The minority brings solutions and concepts that are new and complimentary to those of the majority, thus stimulating corporate development.

2 The possible juxtaposition between majority and minority thinking generates ideas neither party may have thought of independently.

3 The majority becomes infinitely more critical and analytical when minority influences are involved, facilitating more attention to detail and a higher quality of outcome.

4 Potential conflict can mean that both parties feel more obliged to perform effectively, minimalising complacency in both groups.

5 The mere act of having to accommodate alternative points of view trains leaders and team members to be more culturally effective in an ever-changing global business area.

6 Great ideas start underground or in minority groups before going mainstream.

7 Minorities add to widening participation globally.

And all this without the flower-power, "let's all live in peace" oriented, hand-holding harmony that we are taught to aim for in connection with diversity and equality.

It's true that if minorities are included, appreciated and utilised, companies will have happier teams and higher levels of productivity. Variety is also the spice of life, and even for those who prefer the staid, predictable ways of performing usually associated with a more homogenous environment, work would be very boring, not to say ineffective, if there were absolutely no change.

There is also a highly motivating element of diverse team participation for those who enjoy and celebrate cultural differences and the stimulating, exciting working environment they can create.

LEADERS

This has always been true, despite the fact that, in former times, diversity wasn't even a word found in most corporate vocabularies, let alone an acknowledged business area or even department. Yet more and more companies over the last 20-30 years have realised that they are failing to capitalise on vast resources by not addressing the lack of diverse recruitment in their staffing pool.

The result is that, whichever minority one belongs to, intelligently operating companies are at least attempting to create a diverse working environment. They are also trying to consider your skills and potential before your gender, race or physical attributes.

And female leaders are at the forefront of pushing this forward, despite the fact that, as a minority themselves, they can often have more challenges in general to cope with than their male counterparts.

Here now are some perspectives from women leaders who exemplify exactly this kind of approach to diversity and inclusion.

DIVERSITY

FIONA CANNON OBE
DIRECTOR D&I LLOYDS BANKING GROUP

FIONA CANNON OBE

Fiona Cannon OBE is a woman on the move. Fiona has been a diversity practitioner for over 20 years, and with all the wealth of knowledge and expertise she has acquired within the diversity and inclusion agenda, it won't come as a surprise to anyone that she sits firmly within the Diversity trait of the L.E.A.D.E.R.S. characteristics of women on boards.

Fiona is Director of Diversity and Inclusion for Lloyds Banking Group, the largest Bank in the UK. She is responsible for the development and implementation of the diversity and inclusion strategy covering 100,000 employees, 30 million customers and the supplier diversity chain. Awarded the OBE in the 2011 New Year's Honours List for services related to equal opportunities, Fiona cites Deputy Chair of the Equality Opportunities Commission, Non-Executive Director of the Government Equalities Board and the Chair of the Women's Justice Taskforce amongst her public appointments. Additionally, Fiona has been a founding member of a number of employer-led initiatives including Employers for Childcare; Employers for Work Life Balance and Race for Opportunity.

"I am just about to become Chief Executive of a new non-profit company called the Agile Future Forum," commented Fiona, confirming that she is indeed a woman on the move. "I've actually been with the bank for 25 years now. I've always been in this field, so I started my career working for an organisation that was called the Industrial Society; it's now the Work Foundation. But I started work in a unit there called the Pepper Unit which was a women's development unit. We ran women's development programmes. We did Saturday-only courses with Cosmopolitan Magazine. Actually, that was the first unit or department that really started working with corporates on looking at the whole diversity picture. That was about 30 years ago now."

DIVERSITY

Fiona continued, "It was very much focused on gender diversity at that point. But also I worked with, in that unit, someone called Dr Marie Stewart and she started doing the first work around ethnicity and what we need to be doing in that space, which was really interesting. At that point then, it was really a decision about whether to stay in, what you might call, a more campaigning role or to move into something that was more 'establishment', to try and change things that way. So you can't get more establishment than a bank. But also I kind of followed my first mentor really. One of the things that we used to do at the Pepper Unit was run women's development programmes and we'd have role models come in to talk. We had Dame Julie Mellor come in. I thought 'God, I really want to work with her. She was just so brilliant.' So I managed to agree with the Industrial Society that they would second me to work with Julie and she had just started at TSB at that point. She got a free resource and I got to work with Julie. She was doing some really exciting stuff. It was the first real work with employers in this space – in-depth work. So TSB then kept me on after that. And people often ask me why I stayed with one organisation for so long. I guess there are a number of reasons. One was because actually working for an organisation like Lloyd's Banking Group gives you a very good calling card. So people are much more likely to listen to me if I say 'I'm from Lloyd's Banking Group' than if I'm sitting on the outside trying to make a point. That's been very important. But Lloyd's has also been a brilliant organisation because I've done a lot of public policy work as a result of being involved with Lloyd's – they've always allowed me to go and do that bigger work in the national arena, if you like."

ARE THERE ANY DIFFERENCES IN LEADERSHIP BETWEEN MEN AND WOMEN AND IF SO CAN YOU NAME TWO?

I have always found the idea about whether there are differences between men and women quite an interesting question. Really, I

LEADERS

think that people are individuals. So actually you see good things in men, and good things in women. What my experience has shown me through the work that we've been doing and my observations of women, is that there are two things that I think probably are slightly different. The one thing that I've experienced through the merger of Lloyds and HBOS during the economic crisis, and it's been reflected in other organisations as well as ours I think, is that women have a very strong value-set at work, so we need to feel like we're making a contribution, that we're doing something worthwhile, that we're part of a team. The data that I've seen on that shows that actually, that is a reality. So we've seen that women have actually just walked out the door because they feel that their value-set doesn't sit with the organisation. Women are more likely to do that than men if they feel that their value-set has been compromised. The other thing that I observe, I guess, is that women are probably more collaborative in terms of how they work, more keen to get a consensus. So those would be the two distinctions that I would pick out.

HOW MANY OTHER WOMEN ARE ON YOUR BOARD?

At Lloyd's Banking Group we've got 12 board members, 3 of whom are women, so that's 25% of our board.

GENDER ROADBLOCKS, HAVE YOU EXPERIENCED ANY?

I wouldn't call them roadblocks, more issues that need to be resolved, maybe hurdles. They'll be different things for different people. The reality is when you have children, that is the point where you start to have to make some choices. So I guess that was the point for me in my career where I didn't want to work. When I had children I really wanted to be with them and that was very important to me. I know that everybody says this and everybody of course means it as well – it sounds like a cliché. But my children are the most important

DIVERSITY

thing and my role as a mum was my first role. I used to always say to my kids, "My first job is to be your mum". That meant having them, being really full on, ambitious and really going for it. That point was a real moment of truth about how you manage things. So that was the biggest hurdle, I think, for me and the choice I made. I worked part-time until my youngest child was 10. Even now I work flexibly in the sense of I like to take them to school in the mornings and try to be there at the end of the day. I had to make choices about my career. It meant that I was much more focused. True to say that once I got back into everything, it took me a good couple of years to get back up to the same kind of momentum again in my career. But I wouldn't call it a roadblock, I would call it a personal choice, and I think we all have to sometimes make hard choices.

FLEUR BOTHWICK OBE
DIRECTOR OF D&I EY

FLEUR BOTHWICK OBE

Fleur Bothwick OBE is the Director of Diversity and Inclusiveness for Ernst & Young's Europe, Middle East, Asia and Africa (EMEAA). Fleur has been high profile in Diversity & Inclusiveness for over 10 years and has led programmes across large companies including Lehman Brothers.

In Fleur's own words, "I've been in post since January 2014 and before that I had a career that was mainly in investment banking and primarily in Human Resources. I fell very accidentally into diversity and have happily been here for the last ten or twelve years. I work for Ernest & Young, which is one of the big four international professional accounting firms and at the moment I lead Diversity and Inclusiveness for the EMEAA."

Fleur continues, "These territories have about 70,000 people and 93 countries working for Ernst & Young, so it is incredibly diverse and a wonderful learning experience for me on a daily basis." Fleur is passionate about all forms of diversity and developed the UK's first diversity programmes based on race for minorities in leadership. She also piloted a graduate scheme for disabled Interns, and was awarded an OBE for her contribution to diversity and inclusion in the workplace. As well as her busy work life, Fleur is also working towards the opening of a secondary school in Lambeth for students with autism.

"I'm based here in London but travel extensively. I'm a working mum: I've got three boys who are now 15, 13 and 12. My 12 year old is autistic with profound needs. We have a very untraditional home life and it takes up a lot of my time at home." You would have thought that this was enough for Fleur to be getting on with but she added, "I co-chair the Working Families Board and currently I sit on the National Autistic Society's Academy Trust Board as a Director. As part of that, I chair a Board of Governors for a new free school that we are setting up. It's busy but great."

LEADERS

Fleur is the second person that I have interviewed for this book whose faith is in daily practice, as she visits her local church every day on her way into work. She is also a prime example of how to make diversity work in the world of business alongside her religious beliefs. Head of Diversity and Inclusiveness at EY, Fleur has worked in and is very knowledgeable on the Diversity agenda. Having a son with special needs I believe also gave Fleur a better understanding of the diversity strands as a whole.

Fleur is a diversity champion, a specialist in her field. Not only does she focus on diversity and inclusion in her professional career, she successfully manages it at home and in her spare time she lends her experience to make a difference. Fleur clearly fits within the diversity strand of the L.E.A.D.E.R.S. traits of women on boards. This is what she said in answer to my questions around diversity.

ARE THERE ANY DIFFERENCES IN LEADERSHIP BETWEEN MEN AND WOMEN, AND IF SO CAN YOU NAME TWO?

"I do think there are, but I think differences can be subtle and this leads us onto stereotyping. I would not say there is a huge difference, but certainly in my day-job and in the research we've touched on, one of the things which one sees is that women tend to like more detail and like a bit more time to reflect. In addition to that, I'd say that women tend to be better listeners. They tend to be more collegiate so they tend to be better team players, and some of these traits are heightened when the going gets tough; and I fear that the more dominant culture, which tends to be the male culture, sort of suffocates that, or makes it look not as important as it should be. However, that is clearly a big generalisation."

HOW MANY OTHER WOMEN ARE ON YOUR BOARD?

"The board I operated on as my very first ever was really very intimidating. There were something like 15 people, only two of which

DIVERSITY

were female. It was my first ever and it was an awful experience. In my last, Working Families that I co-chaired, we were predominantly female and very acutely aware that it needed more men; at that time we only had two guys. Currently the board is 50-50 which I hadn't even thought about it. But we are half and half."

GENDER ROADBLOCKS,
HAVE YOU EXPERIENCED ANY?

"I'm also not at the tough end of operation. I'm not in a FTSE 100 and because of the nature of what I do and my network, I've had lots of challenges and issues in politics but not male-female. I'm also lucky because I'm the breadwinner and my husband works part time, so when it comes to those challenges that women talk about like being unable to travel, I've managed my flexibility and freedom. I've found a solution, so routinely I don't have to rush."

SHEEKHA RAJANI
DIRECTOR OF D&I AND MEMBER ENGAGEMENT

SHEEKHA RAJANI

As the Director of Diversity & Inclusion and Member Engagement, Sheekha Rajani is a strategic partner for the world's largest accessible and inclusive careers site DiversityJobs.co.uk. She joined in 2013 and her primary role was to support member organisations in the achievement of their Diversity & Inclusion goals, through candidate attraction, recruitment and retention strategies. Sheekha was appointed to the board shortly after joining and has shaped the strategic direction of the organisation and its operating model, contributing to the growth of the business.

Sheekha says, "DiversityJobs is a business working with organisations to promote the work they are doing in diversity and inclusion and to move the needle in that area. I'm new to the board but have been with DJ over a year. Before that I worked with HSBC as their Global Diversity specialist and prior to that I worked with BAE Systems as the Diversity manager.

Specialising in D&I happened by accident. It was identified as something that I needed to do as a specialist, but it has led to so much more through me having the confidence to say yes and taking a leap of faith – it has taken me a long way. Being able to be part of an organisation that makes such a difference in D&I means a great deal to me."

ARE THERE ANY DIFFERENCES IN LEADERSHIP BETWEEN MEN AND WOMEN AND IF SO CAN YOU NAME TWO?

"Differences of leadership between men and women: Having seen mixed boards and teams, I think that both genders can bring something very different to the board. However, I think that self-awareness and the impact that you are having on others – women think more about the impact and step back and consider everything – think about different options and the outcome of their decisions

LEADERS

– they also think about bringing others along with them. Women demonstrate this more than men in a boardroom setting. Listening skills are more used by women. There is more self-awareness and bringing people together to collaborate. Men aren't afraid to be assertive and demonstrate their gravitas. Sometimes women feel a little self-conscious about being assertive without be aggressive. Men don't get caught up in that – they stick to their guns – women don't do that as often, as they try to find a win-win for everyone. Often, it is a win compromise and not getting everything they want. Men are not afraid to upset people to get what they want."

HOW MANY OTHER WOMEN ARE ON YOUR BOARD?

"At the moment I am the only one, out of four on the board, but throughout the company we are currently 50/50 male to female. So board membership can change."

GENDER ROADBLOCKS, HAVE YOUR EXPERIENCED ANY?

"Men are very good networkers and working out where they want to get and who will help to take them there. If you are not good at doing this in a corporate setting, it can be a roadblock. Women tend to think that performing well and being good at what they are doing will get them there. Meanwhile their male colleagues are networking and plotting their paths and teeing themselves up, just like stakeholder management for a project. A corporate structure does not account for that for women, and this can be a roadblock. How did I get over that? I left the corporate world. I did struggle a lot to navigate through that organisation structure and confines. Perhaps I was not politically savvy, not realising who the key political players are. I feel that for some people that kind of construct of corporate structure is not where they can strive and succeed."

DIVERSITY

OVERVIEWS ON DIVERSITY:

There seems to be a difference of opinion on this one. Whilst some feel there is no difference, others feel there is a gap as wide as the Grand Canyon. It seems that it depends on the industry, the type of company, the size of the company, the person leading, and of course, how much you care. There is the opinion that the women are collegiate leaders, and better listeners, but there are also men who have those skills, and some feel that men are more egotistical and autocratic whilst others feel they know many women who have that style of leadership as well.

There is the theory that women lead with circular vision and have more of a 360° view, masters of opportunity, manage and seek good in everyone in their team or the people they work with. Even though they seem to have a more rounded approach, there are still not enough women getting through to those top positions. But here's what my wise counsel said:-

DIFFERENCES BETWEEN MEN AND WOMEN IN LEADERSHIP?

Andrea Wong: My personal opinion is that women are better leaders because we have less ego and are too busy to worry about that. We are also more consensus driven and would rather the whole team buy into where we are going.

Beatriz Araujo: It's tempting to find differences, but I would prefer not to do so because by finding the differences, we end up stereotyping men and women. The difference we all have is personality because you can have a perfectly aggressive women and a perfectly caring man. It's about personality traits rather than gender.

Claire Ighodaro: If you go back to the seventies and eighties when women were not being prepared for senior roles, you might have very much found that they were a lot weaker in terms of their confidence and their ability to articulate their opinions to boards clearly etc. That's not so much the case now because women have far better educational opportunities and are far better developed. There are some studies that say women are better at managing and mitigating risk. So they can bring different things to the board. In terms of basic leadership, intellect, ability to learn, I don't think there is any difference.

Cornelia Meyer: There are no real differences but I think it is very important for women to be seen to be listening and to be seen to be conciliatory. The same traits in men that are seen as great leadership traits might be seen as off-putting in women.

Davida Marston: There are great leaders, both men and women. I don't believe that all men and all women necessarily fall into certain patterns, but I do believe a lot of the good team-leaders I've known were women who concerned themselves to a greater degree in getting to know the people who report to them, understanding their personal lives and issues that might impact them in the workplace. Men tend to be more task-driven and tend not to get quite so involved, and again it could be horses-for-courses and different people adopt styles that aren't necessarily gender-specific.

Heather Rabbatts: This is a subject of a huge debate and what the view tends to be is that women's style of leadership can be very different from men's in that they have a tendency to be greater listeners or more collaborative, have less ego sometimes involved in their style of leadership. So you can see different styles of leadership because of gender but it would be too crude to say that those are hard and fast characteristics. There are men who are good listeners, great communicators, motivators, who are collaborationist in style. So it's about understanding that leadership, and, what is increasingly understood, it is about how you bring people with you, and having that emotional intelligence, as well as the strategic insight to be able to do that. My experience is that I have found that women will often bring that emotional intelligence to the forefront of their contribution and to their thinking.

DIVERSITY

Jo Valentine: It's very dangerous to generalise people, women come in different shapes and sizes, as do men. I'm slightly uncomfortable generalising. Typically women are better at communicating, listening and collaboration. What is healthy is to get a mix on a board. I worked most of my career in fairly mature male environments of one sort or another. It is so refreshing working where I do now with a variety of mixes in ages, sexes and everything: I find that's much more relaxing. There's not testosterone-fuelled egos going on.

Judith Mayhew Jonas: There are not as many differences between the genders in leadership as there are between different types of people. I think that if you are a strong leader you need to know that you have to bring people with you. If you are a consensual leader, you need to know that you've got to be able to be strong in certain situations. It's not a gender difference for me, it's more about personality types.

Karen Blackett: Women are naturally more collaborative and more inclusive and able to build coalitions but they can be as egotistical as men. They feel they have to get their opinions across. It could be perceived as a negative, but women will take fewer risks than men who attend a school of blagging. Women will feel they have to know 100% about a topic, but men will take risks and blag their way as being the expert. Women don't typically do that.

Kate Robertson: Once in position of leadership, I don't necessarily think there are differences between how men and women lead. I think there is a soft interpretation of women's leadership as being more inclusive, more collaborative, more co-operative and more understanding in the work place. I don't like the notion that we're all lovey-dovey generally talking because it's a load of baloney… it holds us back. I don't think we lead in business differently and definitely not in politics. Fatima Bhutto said at a summit, about her aunt, Benazir Bhutto, and Indira Gandhi and a whole range of other people, they were terrifying – they never cried, they made other people cry, so I don't think we act differently once we are leading.

Kristen English: It's too much of a generalisation that there is a difference between how men and women lead. In terms of leadership style, I think most women are not as involved with their own personal image and generally more involved in trying to make the organisation work. So to me that's a very nice characteristic that women perhaps work more with teams and building them. Men tend to be more ambitious or able at putting themselves forward for promotion and that's something women can learn.

Someone once told me that the greatest male CEOs on the planet had a female COO who never aspired but worked at her job so the CEO could go and network for his next job. In its most brutal light that's probably true – you will, however, find some elements of that in successful female leaders. In some aspects women have to act like males if the jobs are given by males. Men are better at giving a hand up to the next generation of men. One thing to take away is that if you want to progress, having a sponsor who is in some sense powerful and helpful, that will certainly help you on your way quicker.

Melanie Richards: I don't agree that there is a difference but we've created stereotypes. There's a great book by Binna Kandola called *The Invention of Difference*, and he talks about us creating stereotypes of what a good man and woman looks like and we shove people into those respective boxes. I've seen men with many of the characteristics that are assigned typically to a female and they are very effective leaders. I do think women and men do come at things from slightly different perspectives, but that is less about their gender and more around them as individuals. I do observe that women tend to be very collegiate. That doesn't mean that they are not competitive. One example of that is that I'm a member the 30% Club steering committee and I've been there from inception. Since its inception, it is true that there has never been a hierarchy or a perception of how we should work. We have collaborated really well. That has been the critical difference and the fact we are all women has enabled that to happen well.

Natalie Griffin: I've worked for both men and women and I've seen really good and bad leaders in both sexes. It's interesting, when a man leads with gusto he could be described as arrogant, a women would be described as a ball breaker. Whether female or male, you must have the quality that people want to work for you. I do notice that, when going for a promotion to the next level, men will tick all the boxes and worry about it when they get there, whereas women tend to be a bit more fastidious about ticking the boxes and worry before they get there.

Paula Vennells: From my own experience, I don't think there are fundamental differences. So if I talk to the male colleagues that I work with, and that I have worked with over the years, they are subject to the same thrills and ambitions and challenges and uncertainties as women are. We all of us suffer and celebrate that range of things. I think the one fundamental difference is that women would perceive that, where there are uncertainties or lack of confidence or doubts, men manage to cover that up better actually. There's something around the macho presentation impact piece to me that they seem to do that better than most of the women and I include myself in that too. One of the points in Sheryl Sandberg's book *Lean In* is fake it. If you're feeling uncertain, fake it because usually you'll get through it. And then you'll wonder why on earth you were feeling uncertain.

Patience Wheatcroft: I'm loath to say there are differences between men and women. I would say there are differences between the ways people lead. I've seen both men and women behave in ways in which they have been transformational and also the opposite. I have seen men nod things through when they should not have done and the women asked the questions. We need a good mix of personalities and experience around the table and gender seems to me rather less important than the mix of experience and ability.

Sharon Thorne: A generalisation is that women are more collaborative than men. There is less individual ego than when dealing with men.

Toni Belcher: I think the obvious one is if it's an unsettled meeting, an unsettled board, or if it's dysfunctional, you'll find men tend to bring in the divide-and-conquer rule. Women on boards tend to be a bit more group-orientated. On the whole I wouldn't say that there are any major differences in that sense. Everyone generally shows the same commitment level and powers of decision making, the brains, they never change. I think the women I've tended to come across they're either very firm and positive and they can hold their own, or actually it's the opposite applies and they seem to be quieter but their presence is still very much felt.

GENDER ROADBLOCKS

The section on roadblocks is a very interesting one. Depending on who you talk to and their perspective on the issue, gender roadblocks are either non-existent or a very real issue within the corporate world. There are a few strategies for coping with what might be perceived as a roadblock but, surprisingly, most feel there are no roadblocks. If not, where are the women at the top?

Heather Rabbatts: There have definitely been gender-related roadblocks. I'm a mixed-race woman so I think there have also been issues of race. But we are all aware that where you're entering worlds and you are the odd one out, that always causes a moment of tension, if you like, about whether you're going to be accepted into those cultures. And certainly there's been times when I have felt I've had the skills and the attributes for the roles, but haven't been successful in obtaining them and then looked at who had obtained them and feel they have fitted a very particular mould. And I think we all know that when we look at issues of diversity across boards the presence of black and ethnic minorities and women are still wholly lacking. And that's because on the whole the people who are doing recruiting are still recruiting in their own image. And I think the current push to get more women onto boards, a greater diversity on boards, it's also about ensuring that the boards have a diversity of experience

DIVERSITY

and thought. It isn't that we should just be there because we tick a race box or a gender box. It is because what you are doing is ensuring that talent, in all of its forms, with all of its experience, is sat around that table.

Judith Mayhew Jonas: I haven't so much had gender-related roadblocks in my career. That's partly because I was trained as a lawyer and that gives you quite sharp analytical skills and a can-do and problem-solving attitude. Ironically for me the greatest roadblocks have been in what you might regard as softer areas such as education and the arts. The City did not create any roadblocks for me at all.

Karen Blackett: There really haven't been any gender-related roadblocks as I feel there have been trailblazers before me. They have set the path and the agenda, and at MediaCom we are 55% women and with my C Suite board of seven, four are women, so there hasn't been gender-related roadblocks because of the women before who have set the right path. Women are judged for their performance. Gender does not come into it at all.

Kate Robertson: There certainly have been and the problem I had in early years and for far too long was having been born and raised by a feminist woman who was the first female board director of a company in South Africa. I was too long at working to see that those roadblocks weren't there – I just assumed that I was good enough and tough enough. But they were there. I don't think I ever learnt to overcome them. I think I was lucky with my time at Havas with my former boss who was a young man who did not see gender, he just promoted the best. He was pretty unusual, if not unique. The blocks were definitely there; I don't think I ever overcame them. If I had to start again, would I know how to overcome them? I might have taken more time to develop a better set of skills in dealing with them.

Kirsten English: There are roadblocks that you know and some that you never knew existed. Just as you would in real life, you jump over them, drive round them, use different and cunning techniques to circumvent them. You can shut up, and sometimes it's wise to do that, or you can tackle the problem straight on, but this could often create conflict. So work shrewdly. I have met them all the time, it is part of life. Work with it in the best way.

Melanie Richards: I am reluctant to say that there haven't been, or at least I haven't been conscious of them. The more I spend time around the topic of whether there are gender imbalances in the workplace, I suppose I can look back and possibly point to those things. Clearly in banking when I joined, 30 or 40 years ago it was a very male dominated business. But I have had some great sponsors, great mentors and great counsel along the way. I suspect that was my coping mechanism for any roadblocks, so I am not sure that I consciously thought here is a roadblock. I will walk through it or never thought of it as particularly gender related. I didn't ever hunker down – I went and looked for help or sought counsel when I needed to. Life skills are based around communications. When you are struggling with adversity or challenging issues, seeking counsel constructively, with thoughts around how you might deal with things and really testing that out on people, has been a huge part of I think how I've handled those things. What often happens with women is this feeling that they should be coping and that they should deal with it on their own; but finding people whose judgement they trust and who will also provide wise counsel is probably one of the best pieces of advice I could give.

Natalie Griffith: To be honest there haven't been any gender-related roadblocks in my career but at the same time I've not looked for any. I don't think of myself as a woman in the workplace so therefore, roadblocks are, for me, not gender based.

Paula Vennells: I think I avoided them or got around them. What I mean by that is looking back with hindsight when I got to a place in a business where I couldn't progress any further and I wanted to and I could see opportunities elsewhere, then I would take the opportunities as they came up. So I can't think of an occasion where I felt as though I was held back because of gender issues but that may simply be because actually I was impatient and I moved on. So that would be my honest answer to that.

Patience Wheatcroft: Only once when I was a junior reporter and my editor had an appointment to go and see a rather snooty firm of estate agents and he couldn't go, so sent me. When I got there, they said they would not see anyone in a skirt. I do recall saying I would put on trousers and go back, but that was the only time, and it was a very long time ago. I've never felt there were obstacles because of being a woman. There are potentially obstacles for men and women especially if they are raising a family or looking after older members of their families, but there are ways around that. I am seeing increasingly, especially in my sons' generations, that men are taking on those types of family responsibilities.

Sharon Thorne: I've never really felt it in my career, but something that sprung to mind was when I was at school. No-one in my family had been to university, and having a conversation with mum and dad about how some friends were planning to go to university, my dad said, "I don't know why you are thinking that way... going to university is a complete waste of tax payers' money. You are going to get married, have children and whatever you are doing, you will stop." In some ways that was a really good thing as it spurred me on to prove him wrong, and I have. Now he's very proud and I don't remind him of that conversation, but at the time it was tough.

Trusha Kachhela: I can definitely say there haven't been any. If anything, the firm in the last eight years has been taking diversity really seriously. There has been a real focus on diversity. I champion diversity with a lot of women in the firm at senior level, we are keen that it should be so and not the opposite. We are not looking to give anyone any special treatment or giving anyone an advantage; it's about creating and maintaining a level playing field, and for me that's very, very important. So absolutely no roadblocks.

Toni Belcher: When I hit gender-related issues and obviously I have hit quite a few, I sit here not knowing anyone in the construction industry who's a male to female transgender person. I'm sure there are, but I've not come across anyone else so far. It was quite a challenge to say to myself, I'm going to change physicality so that I appear as my true sex. I did that at the age of 40 and in an environment where I'd worked with everyone since leaving school. So there were people who'd known me in that environment for 20 years. Realising it would be difficult to change and then keep my job which I liked, I thought, I've got two chances here, one they're going to agree and like it, or two they're not going to agree and dislike it. So I decided I've got to project manage this issue; I've got to come up with a solution.

I'd work out what people's general reactions would be, who might be pro, who might be against, who might just not be sure; and initially I've got to get the buy-in from the other owners. I racked my brains as to what the outcome would be and there were a lot of potential outcomes, and I needed to project manage the situation. A strange example; I have six partners and they would all have a say in whether they would want me to continue working at the previous firm as a woman. I thought, well, the answer to this is to meet them individually, not collectively, and tell them my true feelings, then give them a period of time to think about whether they would like me to continue working with them. I would give them enough time before it happened, so they could slowly get their minds around it. The only difference is that I invited them to meet me after work and of course the person they met was Antonia not Tony.

I arranged to meet them individually so I could talk to them about my circumstances, about my feelings, about what I'd like to do. I asked them to come along for a glass of wine after work, pretending there was a work problem that we needed to sort out, but of course when they turned up to the wine bar they met Antonia not Anthony. I did this one by one because I thought it just gave them the opportunity to see personally what I would be like, so they could have this mental image of me, and it gave me a chance to be Antonia with them which they never would have experienced. It also gave them a chance to say how they felt and for me to answer questions that they raised. I decided to meet the ones who I thought would be the most conducive first, so I could say to them afterwards, "please don't tell the others what's going to happen next week when I meet them". I met all six of them, and followed the process, and at the last one I said, "Right, you guys must have a chat and come back to me and say that in a year's time, if I've changed, whether you would welcome me. I would know where I am, and if you really didn't want me to be working with you, give me a year to find another job". Four weeks later someone was delegated to come and meet me, they said "We don't have a problem. You earn too much money to lose you." So it all boiled down to money at the end of the day. It just shows you how it works in business. At the end of the day it was money. I was given the green light that day and within a year we moved offices, and at that point of moving offices I decided that was the time to transition. I left the old office as a man, and went to the new office as a women. That would have been my biggest issue. I think the only other issues are that I have had the odd occasion where people have obviously, I can see in their eyes, I can hear in their voice, that they might have a degree of uncomfortableness. But I just have a very easy saying, "If they have a problem with me, it's their problem and not mine". I just carry on the way I am, and I haven't really had any objections or any issues since.

OTHER WOMEN ON YOUR BOARD

From this section you will gather that, though many of the women have expressed that there have not really been any gender roadblocks, they still seem to be either the only woman on their board or one of a very few. Though the Women on Boards report has had a positive effect on many of the UK's boards, inside and outside of the FTSE, we can see there is still a long way to go for women to gain equal or close to equal status.

Andrea Wong: On Liberty Media – only me.

Beatriz Araujo: In the UK we now have 3 out of 8. On Global board there were two of us in my first year, she left and now I am the only one. But we are working hard for change.

Carole Stone: On YouGovStone, as soon as I had the limited company I wanted to have women on boards. There was myself and one non-executive. On the Advisory board I had one man and three women and the three women were absolutely brilliant, they were uncluttered by sentimentality.

Claire Ighodaro: On Lloyd's, which is the board that I have been on for a few years, I suppose I am in the lone position of being the only one. However, I should say this, as a board we are forward-looking. Our chairman and I sat down last year and said we really must ensure that we are encouraging enough women to come forward. I mean the insurance industry has been traditionally male and I'm pleased to say that there is a lot of openness now to more women joining the board and we are probably in a process where I would expect that by next year (2014) there will be at least two women on the board.

Cornelia Meyer: None. I think again it's the space. But when you talk oil and gas, there are very few girls around in that space.

Davida Marston: One of my boards is quite small but I was recruited before the Davies Report, so they obviously have a focus on diversity. It's an organisation where the management teams actually

DIVERSITY

have quite a lot of women. So even though the board only has me on it, the management at the senior level does have other women. And the other one is a much larger company where again there are quite a lot of very senior, very competent women in management but I'm the only woman, the first woman on the board. However, I would think that will change as there are further opportunities. They have just undergone a board renewal, but I am sure that there is a commitment to add good women to it.

Jo Valentine: London first – The chairman and I work through who will come onto the board. We consciously work towards 30-50% women. On the Peabody board, there is also a good mix of 30-40% women.

Judith Mayhew Jonas: In the best board I was on there were 50% women and that was extraordinary, but in most cases, in the boards I sit on, the women number somewhere between a quarter and a third.

Kate Robertson: In my board in the UK, there are seven people – just me and one other woman. On the Global board – there's just me.

Kirsten English: Norway and Sweden are gender balanced, but none of the ones in the UK are balanced. However, they are technology male-dominated boards where women do not typically feel comfortable. But it is changing, as women are getting just as adept as men in the new communication world of social media.

Melanie Richards: There are just under 25% of women on the KPMG board; they include Head of Tax, Head of Communications and Head of Public Sector.

Patience Wheatcroft: We are in a minority on both legal statutory boards that I am on. There are two women on the board of FIAT, and two on St James's Place – the other lady is about to become chairwoman of St James Place.

Sharon Thorne: We are in a good situation with women on the board – we are at about 30%.

Sheekha Rajani: At the moment I am the only one out of four on the board but throughout the company we are currently 50/50 male to female, so board membership can change.

Trusha Kachhela: Not as many as we would like. It's a good focus in the firm, but I would say its 10-15% across Tax, but it may be lower across the firm.

7 WAYS IN WHICH WOMEN
DIFFER FROM MEN IN LEADERSHIP

The majority feedback was that our women felt that there are no real differences between how men and women lead. Moreover, they felt it is more of a personality issue than a gender issue. But of those that did mention differences, the following points are the ones that were predominant:-

1 **Women are more collegiate:** We collaborate more, need more consensus, and like to bring people with us when we make a decision.

2 **Women more risk averse:** We tend to want to know things will work 100% before moving forward. We want to see the end before starting at the beginning.

3 **Better listeners:** We take more time to listen to what's being said and by whom before making decisions or moving forward.

4 **Better communicators:** Women take the time to ensure that everyone understands what is being said, and would rather ensure that everyone in the meeting or conversation is included.

5 **Women are less self-confident than men:** It seems that men are far more likely to go for promotion, move ideas forward without full consensus, and generally believe in themselves more than women do.

6 **Personality matters more than gender:** Most of the women felt that differences were down to personality rather than gender.

7 **Women are better leaders than men:** Just one supremely confident lady felt that women were definitely better leaders than men.

7 TIPS TO OVERCOME ANY GENDER-RELATED ROADBLOCKS

1 **Know your legal rights:** The more knowledgeable you are about your rights, and show that you do, the less likely you are to suffer that kind of discrimination.

2 **Recognise the blocks,** what they are and get a skill-set to circumnavigate them.

3 **Work shrewdly, work smarter** to overcome the roadblocks in your career.

4 **Get mentors, coaches and sponsors** who have influence in the company who believe in you and your talent.

5 **Build a support network** around you, and take them with you to the top.

6 **Don't look for roadblocks** and you won't find them! If you tend to look for blockages you will become a victim of blockages.

7 **Move company:** If all else fails and you really feel you cannot get around them, and they are really blocking your promotion, don't be afraid of moving to another company. It usually leads to a promotion in your next job, and I'm sure you are due one!

DIVERSITY NOTES PAGE

List 7 things you have learned and can implement on **Diversity:**

1 _____

_____

_____

2 _____

_____

_____

3 _____

_____

_____

4 _____

_____

_____

5 _____

_____

_____

6 _____

_____

_____

7 _____

_____

_____

EMOTIONAL INTELLIGENCE

"No matter what we do, each instant contains infinite choices. What we choose to think, to say or to hear creates what we feel in the present moment, it conditions the quality of our communication and in the end the quality of our everyday life. Beliefs and attitudes are made of thoughts. Negative thoughts can be changed and by doing so we create for ourselves more pleasant inner states and have a different impact on the people around us."

Dorotea Brandin

EMOTIONAL INTELLIGENCE

"When dealing with people, remember you are not dealing with creatures of logic, but creatures of emotion."

Dale Carnegie

IN THE business arena, the word 'emotion' has always been synonymous with a lack of logic, self-control and/or independent thought.

People who are deemed 'emotional' are often considered weak or irrational and, as anyone in marketing knows, emotions are often thought of as tools used to control people into making decisions.

However, when one looks at human faculties as tools for career development, then emotional intelligence is undoubtedly one of the most important. The ability to perceive, control and evaluate your emotions (and those of people you come into contact with) is one of the most powerful which a corporate stakeholder can possess. Whether or not it can be learned or is an innate ability is still widely debated.

Peter Salovey and John D. Mayer have been among the leaders in emotional intelligence research since the 1990s. They have stated that emotional intelligence is "the subset of social intelligence that involves the ability to monitor one's own and others' feelings and emotions, to discriminate among them and to use this information to guide one's thinking and actions". (1990).

In business, understanding and utilising your own emotions to optimise your decisions, actions and communication with those you come into contact with must surely be a huge advantage.

Despite this, is it still conceived as somehow 'girly' and therefore inferior to a more logical and analytical approach to doing business? It must ultimately be an individual decision regarding the style of doing business (and perhaps personality type). Those who are reading and evaluating the emotions behind the decisions, actions and attitudes of those around them, however, will have the edge over those who are not.

In the 1950s, humanist psychologist, Abraham Maslow, among others, focused his work on how people can build emotional strength, in particular with regard to having a motivational reason behind all actions.

Most successful leaders seemed to be powered by a motivational reason which is highly significant to them and which generates passion, determination and ambition. These are all more important prerequisites than perhaps a sense of knowing exactly where they wanted to be in five years' time. However, passion, determination and ambition are also mainly all fuelled by emotion. If you have the ability to use emotional intelligence as a tool to produce positive emotions and emotional interaction, you will be more likely to be able to direct yourself and others. In other words, you are far more likely to be an effective leader than your counterparts.

Let's now consider some women who have mastered emotional intelligence as a tool for furthering their corporate career. The four featured women in this section exemplify how to use one's EQ to handle everyday work and life-changing challenges.

ANTONIA (TONI) BELCHER
PARTNER MHBC

Antonia

ANTONIA (TONI) BELCHER

The ability to monitor one's own emotions and those of the people around you is a growing skill prerequisite for leaders in every field, from politics to the boardroom. Emotional intelligence, as it is called, is an attribute within the L.E.A.D.E.R.S. traits of women on boards and Antonia (Toni) Belcher shows a commanding range of emotional intelligence that keeps her one step ahead in a male-dominated professional services sector.

"I'm a chartered surveyor which is the profession that I joined after school. I've been doing it now for nearly 40 years. Originally I worked in a practice, Mellersh & Harding in St James's, which was a fairly old-fashioned Dickensian property firm." Antonia continued, "I was born in 1957 in Chertsey, a small town just outside London. I'm the eldest of three boys, with a younger sister. Fourteen years ago I chose to transition to a female. I have known that I was not a boy from the age of about four, as soon as I could think for myself. But being a fairly strong-willed individual, capable and positive, I got on with being a boy. I enjoyed my boyhood with my siblings but I knew all along I was never really meant to be a boy. So being strong willed, I knuckled down and I got on with life. I did reasonably well at school, decided to become a surveyor whilst my father was a building contractor. However, I soon learned I'd prefer to be a gamekeeper rather than a poacher. Hence I joined Mellersh & Harding after school to train as a chartered surveyor."

Antonia has wide experience in the inspection and appraisal of many building types, ranging from large volume/high rise office buildings, mansion blocks and residential apartment buildings to historic buildings, retail shopping centres, industrial property, school buildings, leisure property and housing generally.

Antonia is very much focussed on family. She goes on to say, "I currently live out in Guildford with my partner who was my wife, and

LEADERS

is still my partner. We have three children, two boys and a girl. My two boys have followed me into the construction industry and the eldest works for an architectural practice as a designer. The younger works as a project manager. They both seem to have caught the construction-orientated genes. I see them all regularly. My daughter decided to still do something fairly creative so she's a successful film and theatre makeup artist."

About her work Antonia says, "So now I'm not just a surveyor, I'm also a project manager and I get instructed to manage fairly substantial projects. I'm also quasi-legal in that I'm an arbitrator. I oversee construction arbitration problems. I'm also an engineer which is how I built this practice, along with two other colleagues here who also worked with me in the old firm. The practice centres around acting for clients who want clever problem-solving and efficient, cost-effective prospects of delivery of the project."

Today, Antonia Belcher BSc (Hons) Dip Arb FRICS FCI Arb APM FBEng FRSA is a founding partner of MHBC, which was established in 2007. In her spare time she is a board director of the Chartered Surveyors Training Trust which provides employment-based training for young people often from disadvantaged backgrounds. She is a keen skier, gardener and enjoys travel and motorsport. Antonia is also a fellow of the Royal Society of Arts, and a Liveryman of the Worshipful Company of Chartered Surveyors.

WHAT AGE WERE YOU CONSCIOUS OF KNOWING WHAT YOU WANTED TO BE?

"Obviously, I wanted to be female very early in life. But if you are talking career, I wanted to go into surveying and construction and architecture really when I was about 15 or 16. I never really considered another career. I thoroughly enjoyed it from day one. I think if I'd have done anything else I would probably have gone into the legal profession as I like the legal side of my business as well."

GREATEST ACHIEVEMENT:

"First of all, my three children. I do think it's that. I have achieved a lot. I also think my gender transition. If I go back to my early 30s, there was no way I ever thought I'd be sitting in a chair talking to you as a woman; that's a great achievement. I could not have seen a point in my life where I would be able to be the real me, let alone be the real me and keep my family and my wife, who I share my non-working time with. We're two girlfriends, two soul mates. She had to see Anthony die, she had to deal with it, and I came along instead. Now she's dealt with it. She's a wonderful person. I've got my three children and they're very much a daily part of my life. There are many transsexuals who don't have that luxury, they have to forgo their former backgrounds for the life they want to live. I've managed to do it and work as well. I've changed everything visual about me but everything otherwise is pretty much the same in that I still do the same job. I still work mostly with the same people I worked with before. Moreover, I share the same experiences with them but I do it as a woman. For me it's amazing. And I'm very lucky.

That being said, when I look back and I think, what is the best thing I've done? It's still my three children. The reason I say the three children is because today someone in my circumstances would probably fortunately be able to declare that they are transsexual at a young age. They would then be able to become a woman, maybe even before puberty or they'd have their puberty delayed and then they could ultimately have the operation and therefore they would never have children. They couldn't be able to father children or give birth to them. So from my life, I certainly don't look back and say would I like to be born 30 years later as a transgender boy wanting to change to a girl. And I'd say no, I think I've actually been very lucky. Because I've managed to be who I know I should be, even if a bit later in life. I never went to school as a girl. I didn't do many things through my teens, 20s and 30s as a girl. However, I've certainly been making up for lost time in my 40s as a woman. So that is a great achievement for me and will be one of my greatest achievements."

PASSIONATE ABOUT:

"For me I think it's life; as it was but also as it is now."

IMPORTANCE OF IMAGE IN THE BOARDROOM:

"I think the way I portray myself is the way I convince people about the right path. They employ me to advise them and then to assist them with executing something, and it's got to be done with strength and conviction. If you're telling someone how to spend money, paying someone to rely on a programme, rely on an outcome and you don't have that correlating image, then they're thinking 'well, why am I going to believe you? Why am I going to trust you?' My office is part of that image. We sell services that generate what we see here – success. So it's the same with your own physical image. Clean, tidy, presentable, upright, sitting with good posture, all those sort of things. I know we're in a changing world and I know the young don't come at things the same way I might, but it's worked for me and those sorts of rules I don't break."

EMOTIONAL INTELLIGENCE

CAROLE STONE
CHAIRMAN YOUGOV-CAMBRIDGE

Selma - good luck
with all your ventures!
Carole

CAROLE STONE

Carole Stone is one of the most interesting people I have ever met. Infectious, witty and a born networker with the official moniker "Queen of Networkers" to boot, Carole Stone has spent her working life bringing people together. Being successful at bringing the right people together for the right occasion, round-table discussions, the right receptions, or dinners, for over 30 years is more than a knack. It is Emotional Intelligence, and Carole is packed with EQ, which is why she has been chosen for this category of the L.E.A.D.E.R.S. acronym.

Carole's recollection of her first memory as a child would definitely place her in good stead in her career. "I feel my very first memory at four or five was, somebody knows the answer... and I've always been searching for people to give me answers ever since." She went on, "I went to a grammar school and didn't go to university. I subsequently went to a secretarial college. At 21 I joined the BBC as what they called a copy-taker, taking down the copy that the news journalists rang in to give you in a regional newsroom in Southampton. From there I went through local radio in Brighton and regional radio, based in Bristol. It was in Bristol that I was lucky enough to be made a talk-show producer in network radio. Still based at the British Broadcasting Corporation, I produced 'Woman's Hour' when it came from Bristol for three or four years, along with political programmes and farming programmes before getting my big break to produce Radio Four's 'Any Questions' programme. The programme moved from town to town, village to village, and allowed me to invite the great and the good I felt knew about issues from the world of business, from politics, from media, the mavericks of the world, and I also invited spokespeople from charities to talk about the issues of the day."

Leaving the BBC after 27 years, Carole maintained her insatiable need to keep in touch with her colleagues and the various people she met throughout 'Any Questions' and other programmes by organising little 'salad lunches' at her small London flat.

Pretty soon her little flat was bursting at the seams and Carole would get requests from captains of industry to arrange corporate networking events bringing people together, and a business was born. After reaching the pinnacle of the networking industry and boasting over 30,000 people in her networking database, in 2007 a market research company YouGov formed a joint venture with Carole to create YouGovStone. Carole moved on from London-based YouGovStone, selling her shares, and is now the chairman of a new think-tank called YouGov-Cambridge which is part of Cambridge University.

Carole goes on to say, "I've always thought that if you can bring people together, you can learn from each other's experiences and do things together. And I was lucky enough to do so."

AT WHAT AGE WERE YOU CONSCIOUS OF KNOWING WHAT YOU WANTED TO BE?

"I feel my very first memory at four or five was, somebody knows the answer, and I've always been searching for people to give me answers. So I knew by bringing people together to talk, we would come up with answers to most questions we ask ourselves every day in life. I knew I would be a people's person. I didn't know how, but though I was shy, I knew I would be involved in talking to people. Perhaps that was the solution to my shyness. It worked."

GREATEST ACHIEVEMENT:

"It's loving what I do and having nurtured my friends instinctively. I'm a great believer that you should do things for the right reasons. Don't buy a house that's got a bidet because you think it can sell well, buy it because you are going to use the bidet. I wanted to bring my varied friends together because they would all learn from each other. Those at the top often don't talk to people because they are so used to being isolated. Bring the people from the bottom up. I've always wanted to do that, so I suppose that is my greatest achievement. I was bringing people together to listen to what others had to say and yet I still think I remained a journalist. I then went into a think-tank, sold my business, but still remained friends with the people I was previously in business with.

It was also a great achievement to keep hold of my now husband for ten years before he asked me to marry him."

PASSIONATE ABOUT:

Getting people to talk to each other, and to look at things differently.

IMPORTANCE OF IMAGE IN THE BOARDROOM:

"I don't feel very strongly that you should be suited and booted. As long as you are well turned out and represent your own image, I feel you should dress as you wish as long as it is appropriate."

WHAT FAVOURITE SAYING DO YOU HAVE THAT KEEPS YOU HAPPY, FOCUSED AND MOTIVATED?

"I have a favourite thought which is, 'learn and move on'. I think I feel that very, very strongly, and the only thing I think I say to myself a lot is 'stretch your potential', and what I suppose I could say is that I believe that you regret more the things you didn't have a go at than you do the things you did have a go at that failed. I really, really feel you must try and do the things you want to do otherwise you will be an unfulfilled person."

NATALIE GRIFFIN
COO DWF

NATALIE GRIFFIN

A management accountant by profession, Natalie is Chief Operating Officer (COO) for Commercial Services at DWF, a top 25 firm in the legal market, working towards the top 20. She joined DWF LLP in 2009, previously working at Jaguar Land Rover and Barclays Bank. The overriding objective of Natalie's role at DWF is to maximise operational efficiency and drive improvement in the firm's profitability. They have offices nationwide so Natalie travels around the various locations up and down the UK on a monthly basis, visiting each office. She sits on the executive board and she is one of two COOs for commercial services, which accounts for about £100M of the company's services.

Natalie originally studied business at university, but didn't really know what she wanted to do and did not know where her path would take her. She decided she would go into business, and when she got to the end of her degree, she found that finance was of interest to her. She headed down the management accountancy route, as she was interested in a corporate environment rather than chartered accountancy where you do a lot of auditing. She wanted a wider perspective, and managed to get a role with Jaguar Land Rover and worked with them for four years. Natalie recalls, "It was a great experience as they encouraged you to work in lots of different areas, which helped you to find what you are good at and what you are interested in – where your strengths lie." After moving on to an American company where she stayed for 15 months, she moved up the ladder to Barclays Bank and stayed there for three and a half years. She was promoted into management whilst there. Her duties were varied and she ended up heading the analysis team. It was from there that she was headhunted to work within the legal sector at DWF. Natalie had never worked in this sector before but decided to give it a go, as it was all to do with people, not services or products. She headed up a team which she built from scratch within the firm which lead to her being given the opportunity of being in the COO role. She has been at DWF for over five years – the longest she has ever worked in one company. During that time the firm has had five mergers which she has been heavily involved in and it has grown to 2,500 people. The business has more than doubled since she's been there. It's a role that suits her personality as she likes to have new challenges: that keeps her moving forward. She has been in the COO role for two years – she affirms it's been a very rewarding place to work. There is a lot of responsibility, and a lot of opportunity to help develop and change the business. Not to mention lots of travel, working with other people and building relationships.

Natalie has been chosen for the Emotional Intelligence category of L.E.A.D.E.R.S. because of her ability to work and grow teams, her enjoyment of and expertise in working with people, not products and services.

Her key areas of expertise include:

Driving change and improvements throughout the business to improve operational efficiency; developing BI/MI systems and reports to drive improved performance and more informed business decision-making; leading restructuring initiatives to ensure an optimal cost base and structure; providing a commercial view of the financials and identifying areas of focus for the firm.

AT WHAT AGE WERE YOU CONSCIOUS OF KNOWING WHAT YOU WANTED TO BE?

"I chose my degree because I didn't know what I wanted to be, I just knew that I was at university and I wanted to do something business related. So I chose a business degree that would give me a broad choice at the end of it. Towards the end I still didn't know what I wanted to do. I just took a very pragmatic view asking myself what I got the most from and what I enjoyed the most. That steered me towards management accountancy and I've never looked back from that moment. I was about 21 or 22. It was more about having to consider what I would base my whole career on. I looked at what would give me a passport into lots of different locations, lots of different sectors, as I didn't want to be pigeon holed. It gave me the tools to work in any location or type of business that I wanted to work in."

GREATEST ACHIEVEMENT:

"Personally, a wonderful son and husband plus being happy both at home and happy at work. Also, getting a first in my degree at university when I had my son. I feel proud because I worked really hard for it and got the result I wanted. At work, I wanted to be a COO for quite a few years. It's what I aspired to be, so being able to do a job I really enjoy in a dynamic, intelligent environment and achieving that aspiration is something I feel really proud of."

PASSIONATE ABOUT:

"Spending time with people I love, eating at restaurants, and dinner parties, these are constants throughout my whole life."

IMPORTANCE OF IMAGE IN THE BOARDROOM:

"For me certain fashions definitely count. If you want to be taken seriously, how you look and how you convey yourself is very vital."

EMOTIONAL INTELLIGENCE

TRUSHA KACHHELA
TAX PARTNER PwC

TRUSHA KACHHELA

Trusha is a tax partner at PwC, where she started her career as a graduate in 1994. She leads the Midlands Private Business tax team, responsible for driving sustainable growth in that market. She is also involved in developing the firm's people strategy which involves helping to attract and retain the best talent from around the world. Trusha's interests outside of work include running and yoga. She is also a keen follower of cricket, which comes from her Indian background where enjoying it was drummed into her at a very early age!

Trusha was born in Uganda and came to the UK in 1972, two years before Idi Amin took control. Looking back Trusha recalls, "I have no memory of my birthplace which is a real shame." Trusha recalls that her parents told her lots of stories when she was younger as they had a strong working class background. "They were both labourers and neither of them spoke English when they came to the UK," Trusha's mother worked in factories and her father worked in the government as a translator. She went on to say, "My parents knew very little about education in the UK but they were very dedicated to the cause. Culturally, parents with a two-daughter family (her elder sister is ten years her senior) went down the very traditional education route. I went to school in the UK, enjoyed it and did well. I didn't find it hard. I then went to college and university via an inner city school whilst at the same time being bullied for getting good grades. At university I did an accountancy course with a placement at Coopers & Lybrand, and was offered a position after graduation so I went on to join them."

Never knowing or planning the course of her career, Trusha took each step as it came and did not in her wildest dreams ever think she would be a partner at PwC, such a large firm. Her parents do not really know what it is she does, or how important her work is. It's not a doctor or a lawyer, but they know it is in finance. Whilst they are proud, steeped in a culture of not boasting about their achievements, they never tell her directly... but they do tell their friends and family who in turn let her know just how proud they are of her. Looking back at her career, she can't believe how far she has come.

AT WHAT AGE WERE YOU CONSCIOUS OF WHAT YOU WANTED TO BE?

"I've never been conscious of making a definite decision and making any targets in my life – that's just the way I am. I've been in the firm for 20 years and never expected to be here 20 years after joining. And never in my wildest dreams did I think I would be a partner in the firm. I love the job and the people I work with. I've always said the day I get out of bed and say, 'I really don't want to work in this job, at this place or with this group of people', it's time to think about my options. I can genuinely say that in my 20 years in this job I've not said or thought that."

GREATEST ACHIEVEMENT:

"This has to be getting to partner. I'm very family orientated but even to this day my parents don't know what it means. They are both in their mid-70s and very proud of me but have no idea what it means. Despite this, I do know they are proud of me as they tell their friends, but they never tell me."

PASSIONATE ABOUT:

"The work I do, the difference I make, especially about encouraging women within PwC to climb the corporate ladder."

IMPORTANCE OF IMAGE IN THE BOARDROOM:

"There will be an inevitable amount of unconscious bias and therefore there will be the assumption that your image should meet the expectations of the boardroom. However, if you look different, there will be a lot of attention, and therefore how you use that attention is important as you will stand out, negatively or positively, according to if you are saying and doing the right thing with how you look. As an Asian, I expect to stand out when I walk into a room of white middle-class men. There was a time when that worried me, and that was a lot of pressure. Again this was pointed out as an opportunity, as people will listen to you when you talk… Wow, what a platform. So make sure you are confident and know what you are going to say before you say it – make sure you use it in a positive way. I flipped it into being positive instead of negative – isn't that a good thing to do?"

OVERVIEWS: EMOTIONAL INTELLIGENCE

AT WHAT AGE WERE YOU CONSCIOUS OF WHAT YOU WANTED TO BE?

Andrea Wong: Around 27, when I decided to be in the TV business.

Beatriz Araujo: I don't feel hugely conscious or organised around my life. Opportunities have simply happened and I have grabbed them as they've come along. I feel now, as time goes by, that I do pay a bit more attention in terms of what should happen next.

Claire Ighodaro: I think from a fairly young age I always enjoyed learning. I have always enjoyed school – I know this is odd but I liked school. I knew I liked school, which doesn't make me a model pupil, erm… I am sure that I was as naughty as every other child, but I did enjoy learning, I did enjoy school and I enjoyed good teachers. I am also fortunate to have parents that encouraged me, so I always felt that I would carry on with my learning and go on to university, I would have a profession. I had wanted to become a civil engineer. I loved building, I loved seeing bridges go up – that sort of thing. Of course in the 70s I was slightly thwarted because I was told that civil engineering training places were not open to women because there were no toilets on building sites, so I became an accountant instead, because I was told, 'you like maths, you must go and become an accountant'. But I have to say I have always felt that I wanted a career.

Cornelia Meyer: At about 4 years of age. I wanted to be a leader but more so a political leader than a business leader. I looked at it, I looked at Switzerland, a very small country and figured out, well, there really wasn't that much to lead and I would need to find something else and that was business.

Davida Marston: Very early on. I had a clear vision of the areas which I wanted to work in. I was always career minded and I always had a plan throughout my career of where I wanted to be heading. Now sometimes fate has moved me off that path. However, for the large part, I followed an idea of what I wanted to achieve and I have achieved it.

Fiona Cannon: : I didn't really know what I wanted to do until I went to university, to be honest. That was also partly my upbringing. I came from a very strong Irish Catholic community. I didn't know what jobs you could do. So going to university was a real eye-opener for me.

I've always had a really strong sense of justice which has always run through my life and I suspect that's partly because of being from a very strong Irish community, growing up at a time of the IRA and living in London in the 70s.

That whole deal with my parents coming over, "No blacks, no dogs, no Irish". All those kinds of things, that stuff informs your life whether you recognise it or not. So that sense of 'That's just not fair, that's my mum and dad people are talking about'. So I guess before then I had a sense of being a lawyer – it was in that area. But it was when I went to university and started getting involved in more political activities, that's where I felt actually, for me, there was a real need to be involved in making a change.

Fleur Bothwick: I was schooled at a convent. I was going to get married and be a nice housewife. There was no aspiration for university, nothing. I was typical, never had ambition, you know… wanted to be a ballerina, wanted to be a nurse, wanted to be a florist, didn't know, was never able to articulate what I wanted to be. I only knew I wanted to travel actually. I fell into HR and then I fell into D&I. So I'm the worst role model, because what you tell everybody is that you sit and you plan. My 13 year old has just done a life plan, which I think is quite scary, but they've been taught to do it so they have to think about four different sectors they want to work in, and if so, what subjects for their A-levels they should choose to get there. I find that absolutely amazing.

Jo Valentine: I did know age 16 that I wanted to run my own business. I also wanted to be an astronaut or an accountant. I like working with numbers which is why I ended up being an investment banker. In a way leaders are a bit egocentric which is why I wanted to be in charge. I still want to be in charge.

Judith Mayhew Jonas: I probably began to know what I wanted to be from about the age of 15. I decided that I wanted to be a lawyer, but prior to that, at the age of 10, I decided I wanted to leave New Zealand and live in London.

Karen Blackett: I don't remember a particular time. I do know that my parents were focused on education which I think is a very West Indian thing, and making sure you had a good education which would allow you opportunities and choices. I knew I enjoyed studying. I wavered from being an air traffic controller to a teacher to being a professional sprinter. So I genuinely did not know what I wanted to do until I applied for a job at the age of 21 to 22. I didn't even know this industry and this role existed. It wasn't in my area of knowledge. So I can't say I was one of those kids who had a clear agenda from an early age.

Kate Robertson: Advertising and marketing gave me patience in my 30s. I certainly enjoyed it. I was 34 when I had my daughter and realised that there wasn't going to be another career in la-la land and I had to decide what I was doing was absolutely my career and get good at it. Really, I think it was my 30s, but that was kind of late.

Kirsten English: Not sure I know yet what I want to be. I do remember wanting to be a native American squaw. I think once you conquer one set of boundaries you go on to aspire to something else, so I am one of these people who never arrive.

Patience Wheatcroft: Until I was about 12 I was determined to be a ballet dancer. Then I decided I wanted to be a journalist because my feet were tired of ballet shoes. I did decide early on. I went for an interview with the local newspaper when I was 17. They said go to university, so I did and when I came out I became a journalist. I haven't wavered a lot from that... I spent most of my career in journalism largely writing about business and then I was offered the opportunity of seeing business from the inside rather than the outside.

Sharon Thorne: In my teenage years I wanted to be in Pan's People. It wasn't until I got to university that I knew I wanted to be a journalist. When I started to look at accountancy services, there were lots of things I really liked. So my second year of university I decided that's what I wanted to do.

Sheekha Rajani: Being Gujarati, my caste is entrepreneur. Our generation do not pay much attention to the caste system and not necessarily in the industries according to our caste system. The moment it all fell into place for me was from about 11, I knew what I wanted to do was to be an entrepreneur and make a difference. Either way, I wanted to gain experience in the corporate setting before I went into being the entrepreneur I always wanted to be.

GREATEST ACHIEVEMENTS

It is amazing what these women have achieved and inspiring to see what they think of as their greatest achievements. Not surprisingly, at the top of most of their lists comes having a great family, great relationships and then achievements at work. Here's what they said:

Claire Ighodaro: I have to say I was very honoured to be given a CBE by the Queen. That was very exciting. I hadn't expected it, I had no knowledge it was coming and on receiving the letter, I felt it must be a mistake or be for someone else. Nevertheless, going to the Palace to get a CBE was certainly astounding. I had not thought it would be as moving as it was. I am very touched that those who recommended me for it felt I was worthy.

Cornelia Meyer: I would say that my greatest achievement would probably be on the business side in my builder/manufacturing days in Asia Pacific for GE Energy. Being the only female in a very male domain in the energy field.

Fiona Cannon: On a personal level it's about having a very happy home life. I think that's a personal achievement in terms of having kids, having a great relationship with my partner, being happy, and maintaining those relationships. Very strong set of friends and support, so that's another thing. Then again, in terms of my greatest achievement, there's not one thing, I think, it's a sense of being a part of, with others, changing the way the UK looks and feels.

Fleur Bothwick: My greatest professional achievement has to be my OBE, because it was so out of the blue and because it was for my contribution to the D&I workplace and not for what I have done in my day-to-day job but for my sharing and the knock-on effect of what we've put out there. That's legacy, that's important. But then on a personal level, by far my biggest achievement is winning free school funding to set up a secondary school for autism in Lambeth. It's the first secondary school of its kind, and desperately needed. This has been going on for nearly two and a half years. So I set up a parent

EMOTIONAL INTELLIGENCE

group called Project Vanguard, along with another group, the Hub. We were both trying to do the same thing. There is a mainstream Catholic School starting in September 2015 in Brixton. When we first went to see them they said philosophically, you have to be joking. We have the Conservatives, and we don't want academies in Lambeth, thank you very much, goodbye. But we managed to turn it around, and I approached the National Autistic Society and asked them to help. We pitched in December, we submitted in May, and got the money in May. We are still working towards finalising things, but expect it to open very soon.

Jo Valentine: My children. Then the time that I learned most in my career in Blackburn in Lancashire. I had been working in London and went to work in the north of the country to set up a regeneration partnership. It was alien and small by London standards, with a different set of ethics. I lived and worked on my own for two years. When I first arrived, there was a huge amount of antipathy towards me. By the time I left it was the opposite. I learned a huge amount about how to work with people and get results in that Blackburn phase.

Karen Blackett: Personally – my little boy. Professionally, I would say it is being the first black female CEO within the media arena, but also my time in the agency. When I was the marketing and new business director – I was the leader that won £500M of business for the company. There's a lot of equity in MediaCom for me.

Kate Robertson: Privately, my 22 year old daughter is my greatest achievement. She is one of the smartest young people I know and I know a lot of smart young people. I think I can say contributing to a very happy and long marriage. Work: ultimately I lead on Havas's every global pitch, and I think that was and will remain to Havas a signature moment and changed the network in many ways. That is something that other people would say – that was her. One Young World is to date a big thing that I've done; if God is good to me and he is very good to One Young World – it will be in time a great achievement, and when those young leaders come through, as they will, and lead differently and leading for our best future, even if just one of them comes through – I will put that next to my name.

Kirsten English: My children! If you set the goals and you achieve them that is very satisfying. Misery you can deal with by yourself but achievements you need others to share with. Selling a very troubled business to an excellent new home with customers being happy with the sale, leading teams towards achieving something. Also being the co-founder of a company that went from nothing to half a billion in four and a half years was also one of my proudest moments.

Melanie Richards: Having a great marriage and having kids because, not least, fitting it into a career is tough. I am very fortunate that I have a husband who has helped me fit in a career and was the catalyst for making sure that it happened. I am also very proud and humbled that I've been asked to become the Vice Chair in a firm like KPMG. I am very proud of many of the things I've achieved along the way, especially for my clients which are too numerous to mention. It's a journey which is still on-going.

Sharon Thorne: When I became the first female executive. Executive boards were mainly constituted with white males in their 40s. At quite a young age I was the first female.

Sheekha Rajani: Being on the board on DiversityJobs and the fact that it happened so quickly. I went into the company not expecting that to be the path. It was unexpected – it cleared up some of those limiting beliefs I have.

WHAT ARE YOU PASSIONATE ABOUT?

On passions, I wanted to find out what made these ladies tick, what they are passionate about, and are their passions any different to other women's. Surprisingly, you will find that their passions are the same as yours and mine. It is family, friends and good food. It's the need to make a difference, and working with and engaging with other like-minded people. So here's what they said:

Andrea Wong: People, relaxing and entertainment.

Claire Ighodaro: People. I enjoy what I do because I enjoy working with others to achieve. I am probably very much a people person which is why I enjoy boards. I enjoy different brains coming together, the diversity of the room coming up with solutions. So that's probably my interest.

Cornelia Meyer: Communication between cultures, especially how we communicate with the Middle East and with Africa because I really feel that in the West we are putting that region to one-side. I also feel the anti-Muslim sentiment going throughout Western cultures is deeply, deeply disconcerting.

Davida Marston: Being part of life, being relevant. That is one of the main motivators at this stage for working. To believe that I am making a contribution in some way and it's particularly important to me because I don't have children of my own. I do have two fantastic step-kids, but I think ensuring that you deliver something in life is increasingly important to me.

Fiona Cannon: People.

Fleur Bothwick: Equality, fairness, and respect. I'm particularly passionate about the autism agenda and education for autistic children.

Jo Valentine: Family, travelling, music – Bach wrote a cantata for every Sunday of the year, and I listen to one every Sunday of the year.

Judith Mayhew: I'm truly passionate about opera, ballet and family life.

Karen Blackett: Having a work force which reflects the society we live in. I am passionate about inclusion which is why I set up a friendship programme in the agency in 2012 to look at people who are not graduates and from all walks of life because nepotism is rife in this industry. So getting people from completely different backgrounds and encouraging them to start in the industry is essential. Trying to diversify the industry is what I'm passionate about.

Kate Robertson: Passion: Youth unemployment – gender-based violence – all under One Young World.

Kirsten English: Family and friends. Technology and financial services.

Melanie Richards: My husband and kids of course, but also leaving a legacy for this firm. Knowing I played a part in it being in better shape.

Patience Wheatcroft: Music, politics and family.

Sheekha Rajani: Growing the future generation of business and knowing the value of growing the value of the next generation.

Trusha Kachhela: Female education, especially in India.

DOES IMAGE PLAY AN IMPORTANT ROLE FOR YOU?

Andrea Wong: I think image is important in any role; you might as well put your best foot forward and first impressions do matter so I try to put my best foot forward all the time.

Beatriz Araujo: It is important to try to create a good first impression maybe. Perhaps it has something to do with growing up in the States where everyone is very image conscious.

Claire Ighodaro: Well, if you mean image in terms of appearance and style, that area, I think only in so much that you don't distract others from what they are there to achieve, that's the important thing for me. If you mean image in terms of being professional, being competent, striking the right note in communicating with people, then that is critical for any person to be on a board, absolutely.

Cornelia Meyer: The important thing is to never be overdressed – you can be slightly under-dressed, but never be overdressed. Always be appropriately dressed.

Davida Marston: No, I really don't think that's the criteria on which most of us focus. Also as long as you dress professionally and don't distract from board matters, you can dress how you wish.

Fiona Cannon: Oh absolutely, without a doubt. I think there are three things that are important in a boardroom: gravitas, so knowing your stuff, knowing it inside out, upside down so people can ask you six questions and you still know the answer. How you communicate – so the way you present yourself. And image absolutely, the way you look is really important I think. It's not the defining thing, because if you don't have the first two, it doesn't matter how brilliant you look, but it is the filter I think through which people see you. So, image is one of those things that people often forget about. But I think it's that extra bit alongside those two first attributes that are really important.

Fleur Bothwick: Style is very, very, important. I recently saw a report which says image is the most powerful impression in the first minute, but if it isn't right it takes the longest time to recover from.

Jo Valentine: I have always struggled with how I dress. My natural instinct is to wear a huge range of ethnically diverse clothes which is not typically regarded as appropriate for the boardroom. To a certain extent, once you become a baroness you come out the other end and can wear, say and do what you want. Baroness Trumpington is a brilliant example, she says what she likes, and can get away with it because she is 90 and is past caring.

So to some extent when you are past the glass ceiling and at the board level, it matters less. I was given a strong talking-to by my chair here, requesting that I brush up my business image. There are lots of people you meet that you will have a superficial relationship with and who will never get to know you as a person. They will judge you on how you look.

Judith Mayhew Jonas: Image does play an important part in the boardroom and it is particularly important for a woman to portray the right image. That should relate to what that woman is and not something that she thinks she ought to be. You must be true to yourself.

Karen Blackman: Knowing your brand and being true to your brand is important. Authenticity plays a big part in the boardroom as you can't morph into something you are not. So authenticity is important, you have to be true to yourself.

Kate Robertson: It absolutely does for some people and companies. In Havas Global, if I go in suited and booted and coiffed and punchy, I have noticed that several of the men move back in their seats and think, what the hell is she up to. From time to time I will tip up to work in trainers and dressed down, no makeup. It should not make a difference but it does.

Kirsten English: It does. I think a lot of people can play to boardroom image though. It's best to be yourself. It is more important to some and less so to others. I also think that some people are selected more because of their profile and image rather than by qualification.

Melanie Richards: We all have to be realistic about this. We all know that people make their mind up within a few seconds of you walking into a room, and whilst we do a lot of unconscious bias training here, the truth is that that is human nature and that's how we all are. I spend a lot of time in the boardroom and with clients and colleagues. I think you would be naive not to suggest that it doesn't play a role. There's also something to say about how it makes you feel. It's very rare that I am not seeing a client or going to a meeting during the working day, so I have to be prepared. I also have the sense that I am a bit of an individual in how I dress.

Patience Wheatcroft: I think colleagues need to have a degree of confidence in you, and that's not about superficial image – it goes beneath that. It is important to look smart and look as if you care. If you give the impression that you don't care, people will pick up on that.

Sharon Thorne: Whatever you are doing, first impression has an impact. It's silly to think it doesn't. Even if you think that's not right – it's just reality. Speaking to one of the male chairmen about it, he says if you look at someone and they are not well turned out, he thinks that if they can't look after themselves, how will they look after whatever they are doing for my business.

7 TOP LISTED ACHIEVEMENTS:

- ❖ Children
- ❖ Great relationships
- ❖ Work
- ❖ Recognition
- ❖ Giving back to the community
- ❖ Corporate mentoring
- ❖ Campaigning

7 TOP TIPS
ON IMAGE IN THE BOARDROOM:

1 Image reflects your characteristics, neat, tidy, interested, etc.

2 First impressions count, so ensure they're good

3 Be professionally competent

4 Under dress but never overdress

5 Dress with gravitas

6 Know your brand and be consistent

7 Be yourself and authentic

7 PASSIONS
OF WOMEN ON BOARDS:

❖ Family

❖ Friends

❖ Music

❖ Food

❖ Different cultures

❖ Young people

❖ Education for all

EMOTIONAL INTELLIGENCE NOTES PAGE

List 7 things you have learned and can implement on
Emotional Intelligence:

1 _____

_____

_____

2 _____

_____

_____

3 _____

_____

_____

4 _____

_____

_____

5 _____

_____

_____

6 _____

_____

_____

7 _____

_____

_____

LEADERS

RESILIENCE

*"When you feel tired it means you've tried.
It doesn't mean you'd quit trying."*

Constance Chuks Friday

RESILIENCE

"Business resilience is the ability an organization has to quickly adapt to disruptions while maintaining continuous business operations and safeguarding people, assets and overall brand equity."

Margaret Rouse

AND ISN'T this almost a direct analogy of personal resilience? There is certainly nothing more detrimental to success than the inability to 'bounce back' from failure. In other words, quickly adapt when things don't go exactly the way we plan. It has been said that self-made millionaires lose their entire fortunes an average of 7-14 times before finally becoming consistently successful. This means they bounce back again and again, refusing to accept that the current failure means that they themselves are a failure.

In the corporate world, this ability is even more necessary to survival. It is inevitable that one will make mistakes, misjudge particular outcomes and, quite frankly, embarrass oneself by staking a bet on an outcome that does not win the race.

What one does after this happens is the difference between being successful or not. By now, everyone knows that Steve Jobs was fired from his own company by his board. Oprah Winfrey was rejected by several networks before getting a break. Colonel Sanders' fried chicken recipe was rejected over 100 times before he finally succeeded in selling it. The list is endless – almost every successful individual today first experienced many failures before breaking through.

In terms of corporate advancement, it is certainly true that to become truly good at doing something, you often first have to experience how not to do it, either personally or through others' examples. In addition, there are always those occasions where what happens is completely out of your control and calamity strikes in the form of your worst nightmare. This is where true steel is shown and the winners are separated from the losers because, after all, everyone loses sometimes. The key is to know that you are not a loser because you lose, only because you give up.

As Eleanor Roosevelt once said, "No one can make a fool of you without your permission."

HEATHER RABBATTS
NED THE FOOTBALL ASSOCIATION

HEATHER RABBATTS

Resilience is more than a watch-word for our next woman on a board, it is her way of life and, given her illustrious career and the challenges she has stepped up to, it's easy to see why she is featured in the Resilience section of the L.E.A.D.E.R.S. trait of women on boards.

Born in Kingston, Jamaica, Heather Rabbatts' initial career saw her become a barrister, but this was just the first port in a career path that would see her navigate her way through a number of senior public appointments to become the first woman to be appointed as a director of the Football Association and the most powerful woman in British football.

Heather commented, "My career has spanned a number of sectors, connecting my working life as a barrister with the world of local government and then more recently media. Throughout my executive career, I've combined executive responsibilities with a portfolio of non-exec appointments. And for me, I suppose a guiding principle would be to endeavour to be involved in areas where I believe I can both make a contribution and hopefully a difference."

Heather made her name as being the youngest council chief executive in the country, citing the London boroughs of Merton and Lambeth under her charge. Heather went on to become the Chief Executive of a public sector company, iMPOWER, before being appointed as the new Executive Deputy Chair of Millwall F.C., then becoming the executive Chairwoman of Millwall Holdings plc. In 2011 Heather became the first woman to be appointed as a director of the Football Association.

"I currently sit on a couple of boards which include the Royal Opera House and I advise a film school which is supported by an arts media fund called Arts Alliance. Historically I have sat on boards which include the BBC and the British Council. I've chaired a charity for five years called Malaria No More which seeks to do what it says on the tin. And also the Bank of England. So I've held a number of roles and responsibilities across the years, in terms of my non-executive positions."

Heather is on the board of the most male-dominated bastion left to penetrate, so I asked her which of her strongest attributes she used as her gladiator armour as she entered the arena of the FA boardroom.

CHALLENGES AS A WOMAN LEADER

"I think what is true for all the women that I come across, is that whenever you join a board, you're never given the benefit of the doubt. You have to prove yourself all over again, no matter how experienced you may be. Whereas I think men walk in and they're instantly accorded that privilege. So I think one of the challenges is that. Does that make sense? You think, 'surely I don't have to go through all of this again'. But you do, and I think that is part and parcel of the fact that boardrooms are still very much shaped in the male image. And until you get more than two women on a board, well, most boards are between let's say 8 to 12 strong, you need to have enough women to get to a tipping point where that culture starts to shift.

I think there are different or additional issues if you are a black woman in a white world or if you are a black man in those settings. Because I think if you are a white woman, there are ways in which you can navigate your agenda with your white colleagues that are very different if you're black or from another ethnic minority. You're even more outside those cultural reference points that other people are using."

STRENGTHS:

"I would say my key strengths go back to me being resilient. Experiences or battles, you do pay a price for that, but I think I might have been bowed at times but not beaten. So I would say my resilience is my strength on many levels.

The other is about the point of being authentic – try always to be true to yourself in terms of the way and the manner in which you lead organisations or run companies. Alternatively, what you bring to a board as a non-exec.

I think those would be the two characteristics in strength I would draw out."

WEAKNESSES:

"One of my weaknesses, and I have many, is I suppose at times feeling that sense of insecurity of not belonging and battling against that. I think that at times puts limits onto yourself. As well, I wish I had as much energy now as I did 20 years ago to do as many of the things I still want to be able to achieve. There's all the other aspects of life which play a part as you get older. But I think I'd like to feel older and wiser – and less insecure. But it is still there."

QUOTE/SAYING:

"You can either lay down and die or you can get up and fight! So you get up and fight."

BEATRIZ PESSOA DE ARAUJO
PARTNER BAKER & MCKENZIE

BEATRIZ PESSOA DE ARAUJO

The American-born, Spanish-educated Beatriz Araujo came to the UK for boarding school and then on to study law at Newnham at Cambridge. After Cambridge she went back to Spain where she met her husband and got married. He worked for a bank and was able to get some time in London where Beatriz had secured a training contract working with Baker & McKenzie. They came to London to fulfil a contract and stayed. That was 28 years ago. In the early days she was put into M&A (Mergers & Acquisitions) which was a difficult place to be with two young children (having had her first child at 26 and then another two years later), because there was no technology – you literally lived in the office which was challenging but interesting.

In terms of route to the boardroom, when she became a Partner she was very good at taking on management roles offered to her, the first being looking after trainees – which she really enjoyed. She always tried to take on positions if they were offered to her. She did not necessarily seek them out. She did quite a few and then about nine years ago she went onto the London office management committee and that lead to her being asked to put herself down for election for the Global Executive Committee.

Her key strategic responsibilities on the EC were clients, communications and Corporate Social Responsibility (CSR), and she chaired the Client Service Development Committee. "I was a member of the Pricing Committee and our Business Conflicts Committee. I had a number of client liaison responsibilities and my practice and industry groups were the global (i) Trade & Commerce Practice Group, (ii) Energy Mining and Infrastructure and Pharmaceuticals and Healthcare Industry Groups and, (iii) Compliance Initiative. My EC liaison responsibilities were for 16 of the firm's European offices located in France, Austria, Germany, Netherlands, Belgium, Italy, Luxembourg, Sweden, Hungary, Morocco and the Czech Republic.

I was also responsible for our online commercial training company, Law In Context.

While I led our CSR programme, we introduced a Global Diversity Policy under which we set global aspirational targets for the number of women we would like to see in our partner ranks and our leadership ranks. We also introduced a Global LGBT Policy."

BIGGEST CHALLENGE AS A WOMAN LEADER:

"I always try to make sure that when trying to make a point I check that everyone is hearing or listening otherwise I reword. If not I feel hoodwinked because they are not listening. Rather than speaking louder, you need to rephrase to get your point across. One of the partners asked how I was enjoying being on the executive committee being the only female between seven men? I said I enjoyed it and as a Real Madrid supporter I can stand up to the challenging boys conversation, but, 'If you are really interested, guess what it would be like having breakfast, lunch and dinner with seven women', to which his face went blank."

STRENGTHS:

"I'm very driven and hardworking and like to get things done. Others feedback that I am a visionary, I connect people and connect the dots, an enabler. I put the firm first and am generally very kind and driven."

WEAKNESSES:

"I care too much in the sense that I take on too much. Everything I take on I want to do well, and this could not work if I do too much."

QUOTE/SAYING:

"Every day I wake up and am alive is a good day." Or, "One day at a time" when my kids were growing up.

DAVIDA MARSTON
NED BANK OF IRELAND

DAVIDA MARSTON

By her own admission Davida has had an unusual background. "I was born in this country. Both my parents were English but they divorced fairly early on, so in fact I was brought up in Switzerland, where the rest of my family still live, in Geneva, and in Madrid. I worked in Madrid for my stepfather at one stage in my life. I went to business school in Switzerland so both of those countries played a big part in my life. I've lived and worked in various countries including South America, Spain, North America. I lived in Canada because I worked for a Canadian bank and I also worked a lot in the American States. I have a lot of friends and roots over in North America. My mother in fact was brought up there and I have worked for American companies. So at this stage in my career, I think I'm truly cosmopolitan, although there's a big chunk that's still missing which is an Asian experience which I think if I were young today I would certainly want to have included."

Davida Marston is a non-executive director at the Bank of Ireland. She's had a 30 year career in international banking across the globe including the UK, Spain, North and South America, working with Citigroup's regional head, UK & Ireland, banks and securities industry.

Davida Marston's career reflects her international upbringing. She served as Regional Head for UK & Irish Banks at Citigroup, as well as a Senior Manager at Bank of Montreal in London and Toronto, holding senior positions in the Corporate & Government banking division including regional responsibility for Latin America. Her extensive international banking portfolio includes working in Venezuela, Spain and North America. Her Non-Executive Directorships include ACE European Group, one of the world's leading providers of insurance and reinsurance, an Independent Director of Liberbank SA, Non-Executive Director of Mears Group plc, Non-Executive Director of CIT Bank Ltd., a leading US-based commercial and consumer finance company.

RESILIENCE

Davida's charitable board appointments include: Midland Heart Housing Group, the largest housing group in the West Midlands; she serves as a Member of the Association of MBAs, the IOD and the IMD Alumni Club of the UK, which she chaired for two years. She served as Chair of the Strategic Planning Society, Financial Services Group. She served as a Member of the Guild of International Bankers, helping to develop vocational training opportunities with banks in the City of London. She was a member of the UK senior management team of Citigroup's UK Corporate Bank, and also served as a Director at Europe Arab Bank PLC, and a member of the Audit Committee of Family Mosaic Housing. She is a graduate of IMD business school in Switzerland.

Having been both executive and non-executive, she is currently a director for three listed companies in three different countries. Bank of Ireland, Liberbank in Spain and Mears Group PLC, where she also chairs the audit committee.

Davida defies the saying "what you see is what you get". Yes, she is petite, gentle but firm, and beneath that she has a high pedigree for working on the boards in one of the toughest industries, International Banking. This calls for more than experience and determination, it calls for Resilience which is why Davida is placed firmly under this category of L.E.A.D.E.R.S.

BIGGEST CHALLENGE AS A WOMAN LEADER?

"That really is a difficult one. Gaining recognition for my team: that was during a period in my banking career where we had had a merger. We were the corporate bank, and gaining recognition and respect from our colleagues who had a completely different style of working. You know, the investment bank and the professional market side. The way I addressed that was actually to recruit another woman who was absolutely excellent. She came in from a bank where she had been working very closely with the investment bank and debt capital markets colleagues. She understood the products, she understood the way they worked and she helped in two ways. She helped me train my team to be comfortable in the new products and she also gained the respect of the people that we needed to work with. If I think about it, that was probably one of the things I considered a huge challenge but, once turned around, also a great achievement."

WHAT ARE YOUR STRENGTHS?

"Integrity, loyalty, commitment, hard work. I have a strength which also on occasion can be considered to be a weakness: I am very structured. I was once designated from a psychometric test as a resource gatherer. I have played to that, because the understanding of the strategy which companies wanted to achieve allowed me to use my abilities to think about how I needed to resource the opportunity: to actually bring some value to the organisation. I'd just like to say that on the non-exec side, many of those strengths are the same strengths that play for non-exec roles. However, the ability to understand strategy, strategic direction and to be able to challenge effectively are the things that matter the most."

WHAT ARE YOUR WEAKNESSES?

"I can be impatient. I have a tendency to be risk averse and I'm also very conscious that my style can be a bit too direct. This is very interesting because accepted communication styles between men and women, I think, have a big differentiation. A style which is direct in a man can be acceptable and in a woman can be seen as threatening, so I'm quite conscious of that, but I'm not always sure that I modify it as much as I perhaps should do on occasion."

WHAT'S THE ONE MISTAKE YOU HAVE WITNESSED LEADERS MAKING THE MOST?

"Being autocratic, not listening and believing that their way is the only way."

QUOTES:

"I don't actually have one because I believe I am genuinely a very happy person and I've been very fortunate. I think I have a very happy life but, in part, it's because I've got amnesia about any of the bad parts. When I think back on it I think about all the fun, the good times I've had and actually now is one of the happiest times of my life and so I don't actually have any need for a saying."

ANDREA WONG
PRESIDENT SONY PICTURES ENTERTAINMENT

ANDREA WONG

Andrea Wong grew up in Sunnyvale, a city located in the Santa Clara County of California which is one of the cities that make up the Silicon Valley. Andrea is the eldest of five children and cites her parents as having a profound influence on her life.

Andrea is sophisticated, intelligent, but above all oozes self-confidence which is evidenced by her unusual career path. Her ability to re-define herself and keep on thriving is what makes Andrea exemplify the Resilience aspect of the L.E.A.D.E.R.S. traits on women on boards.

With her father being an electrical engineer, coupled with growing up in Silicon Valley, it wasn't a complete surprise that Andrea took a liking to maths. This resulted in her studying Electrical Engineering at the Massachusetts Institute of Technology (MIT) as an undergraduate. However, Andrea decided to become an investment banker for a while before going to business school and then to Stanford to do an MBA.

It was during her time at Stanford that she took time out to determine what she was most passionate about, and decided on a career in TV. Andrea found she wanted to be a music producer, so having already completed two degrees that were now not aligned to her aspirations, Andrea steeled herself and started over again. "I started at the bottom of ABC news as a PA coming out of business school and making less money than I made coming out of college, but it paid off," Andrea said.

Starting at ABC News, Andrea then went on to work for Bob Iger who was head of ABC at the time and is now head of Disney, doing special projects. "From there I wanted to go into programming and prove I could be creative. I did not know whether I could be creative but I begged for a job on the creative side of ABC and I got a job running the alternative series and late night department at ABC. It is a department nobody cared about at the time in 1998. It was perfect timing for me because I got there and immediately found and brought in 'Who Wants to Be A Millionaire' from the UK to the US, and the department took off. I got to develop shows like 'The Bachelor', 'The Extreme Makeover Competition', I brought 'Dancing with the Stars' to the US which is 'Strictly Come Dancing' in the UK, and I had a great time in that job.

I also did lots of 'Specials' including overseeing the Academy Awards for 9 years and it was great fun," Andrea continued. "From there I wanted to bring my business background back into play and also run a creative enterprise. I got the opportunity to run 'Lifetime'. I became the CEO of Lifetime which was a fantastic job because I got to re-ignite and turn around a couple of cable networks and advocate on behalf of women which was a great silver lining for me because it is the leading women's cable network, and then I came into my current job.

At Sony Pictures Entertainment I have two roles. For my operating role, I run TV production across the world outside the US. We have 18 companies that produce content in their countries. All over the world from the UK, Middle East, Russia to China and Latin America. It's great fun because you can do different kinds of programming all over the world. Everything from high end drama and comedy, to game shows, talk shows and specials – it's great fun and really interesting. My other job title is President of Sony Pictures Entertainment and that's much more of an ambassadorial role for lack of a better word, representing SPE on commercial and governmental issues. That is great fun too as I am constantly learning and meeting really interesting people. I've been in this role for two and a half years now and I've lived in London at the same time. I sit on the board of Liberty Media and Liberty Interactive in the US based in Denver and have been there for four years, and I love being on those boards because they're really addictive for me: when I'm at those meetings, I think really differently to how I do here. I love living in London, but I spend a lot of time travelling. I'm trying to spend less time travelling and more here. But currently, it is half my time on the road and half my time here."

BIGGEST CHALLENGE AS A WOMAN LEADER:

I don't see it as a female leader, I see it as a leader. I would say that people who work for you are motivated by you whether you are male or female.

STRENGTHS:

Dexterity. I can move between having creative instincts, looking at a show and seeing what works creatively and financially, and I can go back and forth evenly. I like people, so motivating people and developing relationships are a strength, I think. One of the most valuable things I got out of MIT is that I've never solved more difficult problems than when I was there. Therefore I have no fear of solving problems. I'm good in the grey, ambiguity doesn't scare me.

WEAKNESSES:

Impatience, and short attention span is a problem.

QUOTE:

"Life is a journey – enjoy that journey."

OVERVIEWS: WHAT IS THE BIGGEST CHALLENGE FOR YOU AS A WOMAN LEADER?

Carole Stone: I think it is taking myself seriously. I started as a secretary and I think there is a danger that you still think of yourself as a secretary. I think I do have to stop myself, particularly as I am someone who is always bringing people together.

Claire Ighodaro: Well some of the challenges one has are similar, I think, to men really, because there are challenges about dealing with complicated business issues, particularly people issues, very often. They are true for both men and women. The challenge I could say that applies to me more as a women would be getting that balance between family-life, work-life and indeed my personal commitments to the community and society in which I live and getting all that into one life, one week, one day, which for women has traditionally been harder. I have three children who are now adults; in fact, I have some grandchildren as well. They are all incredibly important to me, but certainly in the period when I was working my way up the organisation I had to take some difficult decisions as to how I manage my time so that I could give what was required to do my job properly. What I think worked for me was involving my family in those decisions and I am fortunate to have a very supportive family. I think because I have continued to involve them, they have always been part of that career. For me, part of the proof of that is having three daughters who all have careers of their own and have now started families of their own and do not think that there should be a conflict; they feel they ought to be able to manage both. I do recognise it might be difficult.

Cornelia Meyer: It is having a voice and getting people to listen. I tend to listen a lot. But then convincing people that every now and again it is a good idea to listen to me as well, that I find at times challenging. It's very hard then not to get high-pitched or get too pushy. You need, with charm, to get them to listen to you.

Fiona Cannon: This is interesting again. I think it's more about what's the biggest challenge as a leader, full stop. But I think for me one of the biggest challenges is having courage. So in those really difficult situations having the courage of your own beliefs first of all, and also having the courage to call out things which you think are not right. And that can be a difficult situation sometimes the more senior you get actually, I find. So I think that's one of the big things

RESILIENCE

for me, I guess. Related to that as a leader it's about setting the tone and remembering that even if you don't want to be a role model, you are, just because you are in that role that you're in. So I think that's the thing that sometimes you forget as a leader. That others watch you and therefore what you do, what you say and how you behave is really important. I think that, as a leader, is one of the big things that's a real challenge.

Fleur Bothwick: It's what I call micro inequities. It's this whole business about different styles; introverts, extroverts, reflectors. I'm quite reflective so I'm probably better being given a night to sleep on it than to decide there and then. I have an opinion, I will always have an opinion, but my opinion is of more quality if I have more time out. The biggest challenge is not the overt discriminatory behaviours but these micro inequities like a typical meeting where the chair is not inclusive, so they run the board meeting and they take into account anyone who has got a voice. And that could be the person sitting nearest the chair or it could just be someone who's always got a strong opinion about everything and who just jumps in, and you miss out on some jewels from the people who need to be invited to say something.

Jo Valentine: I don't like leading people who are set in their ways and closed minded. So I like to work with people who are prepared to accept new ideas and approaches. People vary hugely and for some people doing the same job in the same way every day is the way they need to work. My personality is out at the other end of the spectrum. I guess my greatest challenge is managing myself to accommodate others.

Judith Mayhew Jonas: The biggest challenge I have had as a female leader was in the academic sector when I had to lead a college out of trouble. That was extraordinarily difficult because I was up against quite entrenched privileged male positions.

Karen Blackett: Females have to make choices that men don't. I have to make the choice as to whether I will attend an evening function or go home to look after my son. That is part of being a mum. So many meetings are at 7.45 or 8 a.m. How will I do that as a single mother? The nanny doesn't start, nurseries are not open. Men don't have to make those choices as someone is at home sorting that out for them. So I have to set my stall out from the start, so that my clients and people at the agency know that.

Kate Robertson: Equal pay is still a challenge. The advertising industry as a whole would argue that there is equal pay but it's actually not the truth. Also women are often not heard. There is a huge communication skill around that. I try to stop it but I see it again and again. I notice that particularly with younger women. When young men speak, they are listened to even when they talk tripe, but it is very hard for women to get attention. There may be parting of the waves which begs the question: "Do you take men with you or are you confrontational and confrontational only?" I almost get to the point where I think that women are held back at board level so much. You are left no choice but to be confrontational. Will that shorten the 70 years? I don't know, but taking men with us I also thought that things were actually OK until I looked at the sisters in the city in the great professions and realised that it is not OK.

Kirsten English: Bullying Men: Men are not specifically bullying women, they are just bullies in the boardroom or as executives, and that is hard to cope with for anybody. If you are in charge of running the P&L, give them hard targets and drive them towards it because these are metrics which make it very easy to see if someone is performing or failing. This tends to manage or curb negative behaviour to a certain extent.

Melanie Richards: We referenced my height earlier, and I'm being slightly trite about that, but actually maybe that wasn't a challenge of leadership but a challenge earlier on in my career – being a very petite female. However, I think I've managed to get over that by pretending that it wasn't true, so the fact I was surrounded by people physically much larger than me didn't really matter. My current biggest challenge is finding time and space to reflect and think. A demanding diary means that reflective time is squeezed out so I have to work very hard to create space.

Natalie Griffin: Definitely juggling work and home. You feel the conflict of being a mother and constantly trying to feel as if you give the best to both. Always feeling that you're never quite giving enough. I don't think I'm on my own on that one. I get the same feedback when speaking to other people and friends. It's something I have to juggle and it's definitely been tough.

Patience Wheatcroft: I think that there are challenges to leaders, not specifically to women. It is very difficult to be a leader on a board – you will need and will have strong personalities around that table, but that's both men and women.

Sharon Thorne: I don't think there is a difference between men and women. My biggest challenge is not having enough time to do everything I want to do.

Sheekha Rajani: I've been recognised as a good listener and being a good listener can also be a challenge. Because you are a good listener, your voice is not always heard. One of the strategies I use to overcome it is using corridor conversations; what you want from the meeting, where do you want to be, and plot those before getting to the meeting so your voice can be heard and you can get your point across; ensuring you will be heard, but heard in the right way.

Toni Belcher: That's a good question. Have I ever seen anything as a particular challenge? I don't think I have a challenge and maybe that's down to me. In the sense that maybe I should have. I get to go to a lot of meetings, particularly in the construction industry where when I walk in the room, there's a quick flick of the eye which says,

"Oh, a woman's coming in to chair the meeting". I do recognise that feeling or that sort of backdrop. But I really give it a very short shrift. So if I'm running the meeting I will just be very business-like and get down to work. Immediately, to stop any tittle tattle. I do like wearing high heels, but running around London trying to keep up with some of my male colleagues when going to meetings, is a bit of a challenge. And the worst thing is if the heel breaks!

Trusha Kachhela: How do I encourage other women to go for it, as I was encouraged? Also having that support around you. I can peg it to two individuals – both male partners, I can honestly say that if it wasn't for them, I would not be where I am today. I would love to do that for other women coming up the ladder behind me. It's a challenge because, as a firm, we have a number of programmes focused on gender diversity and one of the common themes we see is that women don't feel they can achieve it. If I can share my story with a handful of those ladies, I think it will make a difference. I have a powerful story, taking into consideration where I come from. I do see that as a challenge for that reason – I think the firm is very supportive but there is still that lack of inner confidence with the female staff, and if I can share my story and they can see it written down and compare what I've gone through with what they are going through, they can see that anything is possible.

WHAT ARE YOUR STRENGTHS?

Carole Stone: My strengths are really almost my weaknesses. I think I'm non-threatening, I'm not a beauty or an intellect. I like people and I've got great attention to detail. In the sense that if I say to you I will send you a name or send you an article, I do. I've got a reputation for being someone who delivers. I've had that from an early age but the biggest strengths are curiosity and interest.

Claire Ighodaro: I would be guided on that by feedback. I am told that one of them is developing others and if you are going to be a good leader that is actually important. I do like to share knowledge, I do like to ensure that people who work with me are well informed, so I tend to work well with people and hopefully bring out the best in them. Aside from that, I think resilience, which I have needed over the years.

Cornelia Meyer: Perseverance, the ability to communicate well and the ability to listen.

Davida Marston: Integrity, loyalty, commitment and hard work. I have a strength which also on occasion can be considered to be a weakness; I am very structured. But in my executive career I was once designated from a psychometric test as a resource gatherer. I have always been in those kinds of roles.

Fiona Cannon: I think what one of my strengths is being able to engage people around an idea and bring them along with me, so influencing skill. I mean, that's been developed over a long period of time. So I think that's one of my strengths.

Fleur Bothwick: One definitely is resilience and I also put down here humour and passion. Because in everything I'm doing I adore diversity. I'm obviously passionate about autism, I'm passionate about my new school, that's how you find your energy at 4am in the morning doing your emails because you've got this passion and that's the strength.

Jo Valentine: Resilience. I don't see failure, I see things as a setback – I try again.

Judith Mayhew Jonas: I am good at creating teams and getting people to work with me and creating a vision and getting others to work towards achieving it.

Kate Robertson: I am a very good presenter and in our business we are often selling. In a room full of strangers you have to communicate clearly and confidently, winning them over to get the sale. My legal training and being able talk and debate is also a strength. It was an acquired strength. Liking people in our industry is a strength. That would probably be the biggest strength.

Karen Blackett: Resilience. The ability to gel and lead a team. The ability to be able to talk to people of completely different backgrounds which is where a lot of people fail as they cannot relate to people from a different background and class to themselves. I'm good at problem solving, also creativity. To me, creativity is a different form of problem solving, and solving problems is always a strength.

Kirsten English: Honesty, a sense of humour, ability to communicate with people, and target-driven attitude are strengths. Clarity in where you are going. The ability to take people with you regarding where the company needs to go is essential, as well as the ability to value everybody's contribution.

Melanie Richards: I'm very empathetic and quite often I think that gets lost in business. You have to be empathetic as to what your clients may be going through, how they are coping with their challenges and remembering all of the people in life you are dealing with are human beings. They have lives that sit behind the face of whatever they do in business. So being empathetic is a strength. Having a sense of humour is really important. You need to know when it's appropriate to use humour, but at difficult moments it can be a huge tension buster and, given what we are all expected to do, having a sense of humour is helpful and a huge strength. I always have an end game. I talked about having to be open-minded on any particular issue – that's a strength. I think I'm fairly clear minded as to what the end game might be but I am flexible enough to be open-minded – also a strength. Having a sense of purpose as well.

Natalie Griffin: I'm very tenacious and can sometimes be like a dog with a bone, but it also means I'm a finisher. I can get things done, you can rely on me. I will always pick things off the list, and not leave things unfinished. I spend a lot of time building really effective relationships, especially within a law firm. Luckily, it's been with really great people, but at the same you've got to spend time developing those relationships as you have to bring people with you in a leadership position. It's one of those things that even when it hasn't come naturally, I've always tried to hone it. I'm very passionate, I always like a challenge and ways to move myself forward in my career.

Paula Vennells: Certainly resilience. Being calm in a crisis, and being able to get through them mostly. I do have a large amount of courage. I've a good sense of right and wrong. I'm strong, I'm resilient, I'm fairly calm. Another one of my strengths would be getting on with people. I get on with most people.

Patience Wheatcroft: Determined, I work hard. I get on with people.

Sharon Thorne: I have courage and am prepared to stand up for my convictions and challenge appropriately. I work hard, am enthusiastic and have integrity, standing up for principles.

Sheekha Rajani: Being able to leverage the strength of the team. From the point of view of spotting potential and what they bring to the table. It's important to bring out the best in everyone, I am a good collaborator.

Trusha Kachhela: I am collaborative, bring people with me. I do have to be careful that it does not turn into a weakness. If you have real belief in yourself, and I have, you go with your decisions. I also have a real ability to stand back. I can be objective and see what is or isn't working, and look for the right people in the right places to make things work. So the ability to see strengths in others is also a strength.

WHAT ARE YOUR WEAKNESSES?

Andrea Wong: Impatience, and short attention span is a problem.

Beatriz Araujo: Caring too much in the sense that I take on too much. Everything I take I want to do well and this could not work if I do too much.

Carole Stone: I don't prioritise enough. I often do three or four events in an evening and it's quite energetic to go somewhere and only stay half an hour without needing to slip away. I didn't marry until I was 57, so I'm not looking for a new man or even a new job but I'm always thinking what's around the corner, so that's the stimulus of what's around the corner. I'm always thinking, who else can I meet, who else almost might have the secret of life though, of course, you've got to find that yourself. It can be a strength, but also a weakness.

Claire Ighodaro: Always a more difficult one. I would say for me, one of them which I watch is taking on too much. I believe the adage "if you want something done, give it to a busy person" but again, in order to do things properly one has to be careful and manage one's time so you can give adequate attention to what you are doing. I do tend to be more careful nowadays not to take on as much as I can, but as much as I can do.

Cornelia Meyer: I sometimes talk too much.

Davida Marston: Well, I can be impatient. I have a tendency to be risk averse and also I'm very conscious that my style can be a bit too direct. That's very interesting because communication style which is direct in a man can be acceptable and in a woman can be seen as threatening, so I'm quite conscious of that but I'm not always sure that I modify it as much as I perhaps should do on occasion.

Fiona Cannon: My big weakness and my team will absolutely attest to this is, I'm just too impatient. So I always want it done.

RESILIENCE

Everything's always urgent because it matters to try and get things done. So that is a big weakness point.

Fleur Bothwick: My weakness is I do take it all very personally, so you know that is an area. I don't know if it is a female thing, but I can hear the advice but I think it's all very personal to me.

Jo Valentine: I'm very confident in going in the direction I want to, and as a result less accommodating and tolerant of people who are not open-minded. I think it's called emotional intelligence.

Judith Mayhew Jonas: I make decisions far too quickly and I am often impatient. I do get very frustrated if I know what is right is being blocked by others.

Karen Blackett: I don't have the ability to switch off easily, I take things really seriously, so I can be a bit of a hard task master, as I want to get things right and get them done. So I can be driven. Sometimes you just need to let things go. I have a poster saying "Done Is Better Than Perfect" which reminds me that perfection is great but not always achievable. So I would say that is a weakness.

Kate Robertson: Wanting to be liked? Impatience with detail, a huge failing and I think for too long I've told myself I was good at detail. I don't have so much now, but I used to have a great photographic memory. Detail is everything, absolutely everything. Mastery of it defines and separates the women from the girls and the men from the boys. It's impatience with it. The best thing I had but I have squandered is the ability to look at something and say that is the solution, but because I am so impatient with the details I cannot get people to go where I went.

Kirsten English: If you are too focused on your goal you can sometimes forget the people angle. Perhaps one of the ways to compensate that is to remember that people are not successful, teams are successful.

Melanie Richards: Caring too much. I'm not sure you can care too much and being very passionate about things which can manifest itself in not being objective enough. I've learned to manage my passions.

Natalie Griffin: Impatience. I have a short attention span, which is probably why this is the longest I've ever worked anywhere, but it's also the happiest I've ever been anywhere. That's because there's so much to do here and lots of things to get my teeth into. If I was to stagnate in a role, I would just move roles or businesses.

Paula Vennells: I suppose actually one of the strengths is also one of my weaknesses. I either want to go too broad or too deep and get too interested in things, when actually I should back off and let other colleagues do that. It's mostly out of an interest to learn or a desire to help get to a solution on something. But sometimes just going in too far is, I know, something I have to be very aware of. And another one would be not saying no often enough.

Patience Wheatcroft: I am very determined which can sometimes be difficult – my husband would tell you I'm stubborn which amounts to the same thing. I can also be a bit of a perfectionist. I think everyone has to be pragmatic and sometimes settle for adequate and good, rather than always striving for excellence and failing.

Sharon Thorne: I am a perfectionist which, when you have too much to do, is not good. I can be impatient when I am busy.

Sheekha Rajani: My own limiting beliefs, which always seem to be there. I need to have confidence in what I am doing and realise that I do know what I am doing now.

Toni Belcher: Cars.

Trusha Kachhela: Women tend to be more collaborative. I can sometimes be so collaborative that I have the inability to be more decisive. There is no right or wrong, but generally women tend to look for consensus. That can be a strength and it can also be a weakness.

RESILIENCE

QUOTES: DO YOU HAVE A FAVOURITE SAYING THAT HELPS TO KEEP YOU HAPPY, FOCUSED, OR MOTIVATED?

Beatriz Araujo: "Every day I wake up and I am alive is a good day", or "One day at a time".

Carole Stone: I have a favourite thought which is, 'learn and move on'. I think I feel that very, very strongly. and the only thing I think I say to myself a lot is 'stretch your potential', What I suppose I could say is that I believe that "you regret more the things you didn't have a go at than you do the things you did have a go at that failed". I really, really feel you must try and do the things you want to do otherwise you will be an unfulfilled person.

Cornelia Meyer: Churchill, "Never, never, never give up".

Fleur Bothwick: "This moment will pass."

Heather Rabbatts: "You can either lay down and die or you can get up and fight! So get up and fight."

Judith Mayhew Jonas: I think the saying that I cling onto the most is the one that you should "seize every opportunity and make the most of it".

Karen Blackett: "Doing is better than perfect" and "Just keep going".

Kate Robertson: "Count your blessings."

Kirsten English: "Through adversity you reach the stars."

Melanie Richards: Winston Churchill said, "If you're going through hell – keep going!" It sounds negative, but actually there are moments you need to be reminded – just keep going. Also, "You are never too old to set a new goal or dream a new dream!"

Patience Wheatcroft: Favourite saying: "Seize the day."

Sharon Thorne: Saying: "Life is very short – so make the most of it – whatever you're doing."

Sheekha Rajani: "It will be alright on the night." I worry a lot – always worrying about meetings, pitches and presentations. I have to remind myself it will be alright on the night.

Toni Belcher: "Never assume or presume."

Trusha Kachhela "Is this going to matter in six months' time?" It actually really does help me as I can look at it more objectively and not in the heat of the moment. Will it really be an issue?

7 CHALLENGES YOU
MIGHT FACE ON A BOARD

1 **Andrea Wong:** Don't see it as a female leader, see it as a leader. People who work for you are motivated by you whether you are male or female.

2 **Claire Ighodaro:** The challenge that applies to women would be getting that balance between work-life and personal commitments to the community and society.

3 **Karen Blackett:** Females have to make the hard choices that men don't. I have to make the choice between attending an evening function or going home to look after my son. That is part of being a mum. Many meetings are at 7.45am or 8am when the Nanny hasn't started, nurseries are not open. How do I do that as a single mother?

4 **Kate Robertson:** Equal pay is still a challenge. Also women are often not heard. I also thought it was OK until I looked at the sisters in the great professions.

5 **Kirsten English:** Bullying Men: Men are not specifically bullying women, they are just bullies in the boardroom or as executives, and that is hard to cope with for anybody.

RESILIENCE

6 **Natalie Griffin:** Definitely juggling work and home. You feel the conflict of being a mother and constantly trying to feel as if you give the best to both. Always feeling that you're never quite giving enough.

7 **Trusha Kachhela:** How do I encourage other women to go for it as I was encouraged? Also having that support around you to achieve that.

7 STRENGTHS YOU MIGHT NEED TO BE ON BOARDS

1 **Carole Stone:** Like people, great attention to detail, have a reputation for being someone who delivers, also curiosity and interest.

2 **Cornelia Meyer:** Perseverance, the ability to communicate well and the ability to listen.

3 **Fleur Bothwick:** Definitely resilience, humour and passion.

4 **Jo Valentine:** Resilience. I don't see failure, I see things as a setback – I try again.

5 **Judith Mayhew Jonas:** Be good at creating a vision and getting a team to work towards achieving it.

6 **Melanie Richards:** Be empathetic to colleagues and clients – this is a strength. Having a sense of humour is really important. Be clear what the end game might be but be flexible enough to be open-minded, which is also a strength. Having a sense of purpose.

7 **Natalie Griffin:** Spend time building effective relationships within your firm. Be a finisher, get things done. Be passionate, challenge yourself in your career.

BONUS STRENGTH:

Sharon Thorne: Have courage, stand up for your convictions and challenge appropriately. Work hard enthusiastically, and have integrity and principles.

7 WEAKNESSES TO BE
AWARE OF ON BOARDS

1 **Fleur Bothwick:** Don't take it all very personally. I can hear the advice but I think it's all very personal to me.

2 **Jo Valentine:** Being too confident going in the direction you want to, and as a result less accommodating and tolerant of people who are not open-minded. I think it's called emotional intelligence.

3 **Kirsten English:** If you are too focused on your goal you can sometimes forget the people angle. People are not successful, teams are successful.

4 **Melanie Richards:** Caring too much. Learn to manage your passions.

5 **Patience Wheatcroft:** Being very determined can sometimes be difficult. Also, being too much of a perfectionist. I think everyone has to be pragmatic and sometimes settle for adequate and good rather than always striving for excellence and failing.

6 **Sheekha Rajani:** One's own limiting beliefs, which can often to be there. You need to have confidence in what you are doing and realise that you do know what you are doing now.

7 **Trusha Kachhela:** Women tend to be more collaborative. It can sometimes be so collaborative that you have the inability to make decisions. There is no right or wrong, but generally women tend to look for consensus. That can be a strength and can be a weakness.

7 QUOTES THAT MIGHT MOTIVATE YOU AND KEEP YOU FOCUSED

1 "Life is very short, so make the most of it, and enjoy whatever you're doing."
Sharon Thorne.

2 "Seize the day."
Baroness Patience Wheatcroft.

3 "Winston Churchill said, 'If you're going through hell, keep going!' There are moments you need to be reminded to just keep going."
Melanie Richards.

4 "Through Adversity you can reach the stars."
Kirsten English.

5 "Life can be a long journey so enjoy the ride."
Andrea Wong.

6 " 'This too will pass.' For the tough moments."
Fleur Bothwick.

7 "Never presume or assume."
Toni Belcher.

LEADERS

RESILIENCE NOTES PAGE

List 7 things you have learned and can implement on **Resilience**:

1 _____
_____
_____

2 _____
_____
_____

3 _____
_____
_____

4 _____
_____
_____

5 _____
_____
_____

6 _____
_____
_____

7 _____
_____
_____

SIDEBAR

SIDEBAR

THIS IS the chapter that looks at habits of these powerful women which act as counter-balances to their shrewd business acumen. It provides a useful insight as to how these women on boards think. I wanted to find out a bit more about the women, at work, rest and play and what makes them tick.

For the Sidebar chapter we asked the following quick fire questions, and the answer could be as short or as long as they felt necessary.

WHAT TIME DO YOU WAKE UP/GO TO BED?

There really wasn't a scientific answer to this question but given that we all had the same 24 hours in a day to make a difference, I wanted to know what they did with the times when they were not at the office. I wanted to know what time zone they were in at any one time, and what their travel plans were that day. What I found useful was that the waking times of the women on boards interviewed ranged between 4.30am and 7am.

Going to bed was again what might be expected and generally ranged between 10.30pm and midnight. Though there were a few who might retire by 9.30pm, and the other extreme was 1am. There were also one or two who believed in the Margaret Thatcher theory that you only needed 4 hours of sleep a day, but over a lengthy period of time – as one might agree – sleep deprivation does not bode well in the end.

WHAT DO YOU DO IN THE FIRST HOUR OF WAKING?

Again a range of things you might expect, and some you might not. From saying a prayer, having a cup of coffee to wake up, showering, reading overnight emails, gym for an hour, yoga, run, reading papers, reading twitter news headline, prepping for the day's appointments and travel; and for those with children, prepping breakfast for them, getting them off to, or dropping them at school or nursery. Sounds like a whole day's work before they even got there.

WHAT MUST YOU CARRY IN YOUR HANDBAG EVERY DAY?

Must haves include: money, phones, keys, lip gloss, hairbrush and perfume. Can do without: full make-up bag.

Definitely the girlie things you might expect, but 98% of them must have make-up but more so lip gloss or lip stick without fail. To quote one: "Red lipstick is a must, it's like my gladiator suit when going to meetings, they know I mean business, I can face the world." All must have money – not necessarily cash; they must all have phones – this has all their life on it – can't do without. Most must have a hairbrush, all must have house keys, and some must have perfume, the spray-on confidence. All except for one person – Jo Valentine being the free spirited person she is – she does have a handbag! And guess what the surveyor carries in her handbag… a torch, a tape measure, a cheque book and a marble! Want to know why a marble? Visit our website for the full story.

LEADERS

SOCIAL MEDIA ACCOUNTS

Surprisingly, as many of them do not personally or individually have social media accounts as those who do. The least popular amongst women on boards is Facebook, Twitter and Google+. Most do not use YouTube, and few have Instagram accounts. The best used is LinkedIn, where it seems the majority have an account. No other social media were mentioned during the interviews.

WHAT MUST YOU START DOING?

Andrea Wong: Resting more.

Beatriz Araujo: Being realistic about what I agree to do, and don't agree to do, too much.

Carole Stone: Cut down bringing people together.

Claire Ighodaro: Relaxing. I didn't list you all the boards I'm on. Perhaps at one point in the future of my life I will do a little bit less. I don't feel tired yet, but the time might come.

Cornelia Meyer: Having more confidence in myself.

Davida Marston: I'd like to put into practice a bit more of the travel plans I've been delaying. It would be absolutely fantastic to start exploring parts of the world.

Fiona Cannon: I need to start doing more exercise. More drama classes, because this field can be quite dramatic as well.

Fleur Bothwick: Sleep more.

Heather Rabbatts: Sleeping more. I'm a terrible sleeper.

Jo Valentine: Make better speeches.

Judith Mayhew Jonas: Plan, and to have good strategic vision.

Karen Blackett: Making sure I'm in the gym at least three times a week. It's important.

Kate Robertson: Hold on to the knowledge that all will be well.

Kirsten English: Focusing more on my next aspiration, maybe to chair a company.

Melanie Richards: Start dancing.

Natalie Griffin: Spending more time with my direct team, as the business evolves.

Patience Wheatcroft: Being better organized.

Paula Vennells: Actually it's more what I need to restart doing which is doing something else after 8 o'clock at night. I have a habit of doing emails on the train on the way home, getting home, having supper and then opening up the iPad again which is terrible, and I had a New Year's resolution this year which I kept until the end of April, which was not to do any emails after 8 o'clock at night and I've just resurfaced it, so I've got a note stuck in my kitchen at the moment saying no emails after 8 o'clock.

Sharon Thorne: Celebrate making it to 50 and be happy.

Sheekha Rajani: Spreading the message and paying it forward.

Toni Belcher: I need to go back to doing my pilates. I like being fit but I find that as I get older I'm less supple and pilates is a really good way to keep supple. I'd like to say I'm a keen skier. I used to go heli-skiing. Once a year I go to Canada and I do a couple of weeks' heli-skiing. And for heli-skiing you need good core, and pilates did help my core.

Trusha Kachhela: My Next Phase.

WHAT MUST YOU STOP DOING?

Andrea Wong: Can't say right now.

Beatriz Araujo: Having too high expectations of myself and others.

Carole Stone: Bringing people together.

Claire Ighodaro: I have hopefully over the years stopped doing a number of things that I felt were going wrong so I don't point to individual things that I stop doing. What I hope to do again is to enhance the things I hope I am doing right.

Cornelia Meyer: Talk so much.

Davida Marston: Oh well, my husband says I have to stop being on my iPad and my laptop at all times of the day and night. It drives him batty.

Fiona Cannon: I need to stop micro-managing my team.

Fleur Bothwick: For me, stop saying yes. This is my 2014… I hate saying no but I have to be more measured.

Heather Rabbatts: Worrying about stuff I can't change.

Jo Valentine: Stop working so hard but would be bored the minute I do. Not micro-manage the team.

Judith Mayhew Jonas: I think it is really sad when a board spends its time micro-managing executives and not undertaking the really important roles of the non-exec, strategic thinking, good governance, financial accountability, managing stakeholder interests, and boards begin to fail when what they do all the time is simply second-guess the executive team.

Karen Blackett: Reading emails at midnight.

Kate Robertson: Being afraid.

Melanie Richards: Saying yes to everyone, so manage time better.

Natalie Griffin: Having so many things to do. Stop taking so many meetings, be more structured and leave myself some time.

Patience Wheatcroft: Being disorganised and double booking.

SIDEBAR

Paula Vennells: I wrote down doubting myself. So that's the flip, the flip side of that.

Sharon Thorne: Stop being self-critical. Less rushing around.

Sheekha Rajani: Limiting beliefs.

Trusha Kachhela: Worrying too much.

WHAT MUST YOU KEEP DOING?

Andrea Wong: Improving.

Beatriz Araujo: Being positive and looking for challenges.

Carole Stone: Bringing people together.

Claire Ighodaro: Carry on learning until I am very old and wrinkly.

Cornelia Meyer: Strive to always be your best and give your best to every situation.

Davida Marston: Enjoying life. You know this isn't a rehearsal.

Fiona Cannon: Keep listening to the voices that are important in my work.

Fleur Bothwick: Networking.

Heather Rabbatts: Stay curious about the world and all of its weird and wonderful manifestations.

Jo Valentine: Trying to do better.

Judith Mayhew Jonas: Always look forward and see where you are going and where the company is going and not get too tied down with just day-to-day activities.

Karen Blackett: Learning.

Kate Robertson: Staying focused and determined.

Kirsten English: Playing sport, squash and tennis.

Melanie Richards: Energy and enthusiasm that gives you the power to change things.

Natalie Griffin: Enjoying my role, never forgetting the ability I have to change the shape of not only the business but my own role.

Patience Wheatcroft: Must keep doing: Touching my toes.

Paula Vennells: Believing in myself and continuing to push. Because this is a very big business, it's coming from something that is rooted in a particular type of culture which we are trying to change. And you can't flip it like that overnight but you do have to continue to push it and stretch it to where I think it can go.

Sharon Thorne: Keep having fun is really important. I've been learning to breathe properly.

Sheekha Rajani: Must continue to be focused, and leverage on the skills in the team.

Toni Belcher: Keep working to help others. I do a fair bit for the elderly people in the community and I do a fair bit for surveying, the training side of surveying, trying to help disadvantaged people. I would like to think I would continue doing that. But also I love spending time with my family. Being a property person I've bought some interesting property and I have a nice old vicarage in France which I've restored and I have a new, modern villa down in the south of Italy that I designed and had built. So I try to sneak off to those two properties whenever I have a chance.

Trusha Kachhela: Keep being grounded.

HOW DO YOU UNWIND?

Whilst there were some, I expected more high-powered sport and activities, such as skiing, running marathons, golf, diving. But no

— again they are mostly just like you and me. Here's what highly successful women on boards do to unwind, relax and de-stress.

Andrea Wong: Read, watch TV and movies.

Carole Stone: Sit quietly, meditate and let my mind amble and let a new idea come into it.

Claire Ighodaro: Nice quiet walks by the river. I'm lucky enough to live reasonably near the Thames. I have lovely walks along it and sometimes with my little grandsons. It's great and I still enjoy feeding the ducks.

Cornelia Meyer: I horse ride regularly.

Davida Marston: Play golf badly. I play tennis slightly less badly. Really spending time with friends which I don't have enough time in the UK but I have quite a lot in Florida where we have a home so that to me is the top of the list, and I love reading as well. It's a real pleasure to read something that isn't a board document.

Fiona Cannon: At weekends I play tennis with my sons and run with my daughter:

Fleur Bothwick: I spend a lot of time doing stuff outside of the day job so I do have a significant balance now. To the average person it might sound bizarre that I'm doing a Free School, but to unwind from the day-job, oh my gosh, it's a different world. And my joy, that I spend all my free time with the children.

Heather Rabbatts: I see my friends. Go walking probably, walking my dogs.

Jo Valentine: Playing the piano, singing with the children, playing Candy Crush, playing bridge, killer stick, and eating wonderful meals that my husband cooks.

Judith Mayhew Jonas: I unwind by indulging in what I really enjoy most and that is music, ballet, opera and gardening.

Karen Blackett: My son is a brilliant tonic to stuff that goes on in the day – so talking to a 4 year old makes you put things in perspective. Spending time with him – going to a cricket match, horse riding.

Kate Robertson: Read, watch telly endlessly. Growing up in Apartheid, we did not have a television so I'm catching up. I go to the gym a lot, it does help you unwind.

Kristen English: Sport – and as you get older there are children in your life so more time should be spent with family.

Melanie Richards: Running, theatre quite a lot – pilates, watching my son play cricket.

Natalie Griffin: Cooking and reading is cathartic. Being with husband and son, travelling and seeing the world and being with friends, shopping with mum. Important to have that balanced time in diary for friends and family as well as work.

Patience Wheatcroft: Opera. I go to the Italian Opera every year – three operas in three nights. Granddaughter – time with her is absolute bliss.

Paula Vennells: A little bit of running. You can take a pair of running shoes wherever you go. My husband and I go out cycling, usually twice most weekends. I've got the most fantastic Italian road bike which is really, really lightweight and no using gears on it. It can go uphill backwards. I love the fresh air. I was brought up in Manchester on the edge of the Peak District and bliss for me is hillwalking – and I live in Bedfordshire where there's no hills. So cycling is the closest I can get. And being with the family, and church.

Sharon Thorne : Take the dogs for long walks.

Sheekha Rajani: I spend time with family and friends.

Toni Belcher: Gardening.

Trusha Kachhela: Exercise, running, yoga.

SIDEBAR

SIDEBAR NOTES PAGE

List 7 things you have learned and can implement on
habits of highly successful women on boards:

1 _____
_____
_____

2 _____
_____
_____

3 _____
_____
_____

4 _____
_____
_____

5 _____
_____
_____

6 _____
_____
_____

7 _____
_____
_____

REFERENCES

THE BOOKS LEADERS READ:

The Divine Comedy by 13ᵗʰ century Italian writer Dante Alighieri

Citizen Quinn by Ian Kehoe and Gavin Daly

Enron: The Smartest Guys in the Room
by Bethany McLean and Peter Elkind

Fool's Gold by Gillian Tett

Life After Life by Kate Atkinson

Organising Genius by Warren Bennis

The 30 Lies About Money by Peter Koenig

Daughter of the Forest by Juliet Marillier

How to Build a Habitable Planet
 by Charles H Longmuir and Wally Broecker

I Stand Corrected by Eden Galley

Lean In by Sheryl Sandberg

Long Walk To Freedom by Nelson Mandela

Quiet by Susan Cain

Stoner by John Edward Williams

Tell The Truth by Sue Unerman

The Girl Who Kicked the Hornet's Nest by Stieg Larsson

The Kite Runner by Khalid Hosseini

The Lie by Helen Dunmore

The Little Coffee Shop of Kabul by Deborah Rodriguez

The Pirate Inside by Adam Morgan,

The Snow Goose by William Fiennes.

The Unlikely Pilgrimage of Fry by Rachael Joyce.

The Value of Difference by Binna Kandola.

Transitions by William Bridges.

Ulysses by James Joyce

Hard Choices by Hillary Clinton

I Claudius by Robert Graves

Leading at the Edge: Leadership Lessons from the Extraordinary Saga of Shackleton's Antarctic Expedition by Dennis Perkins, Margaret Holtman, Paul Kessler, Catherine Mccarthy

The Chimp Paradox by Dr Steve Peters

The Hare with Amber Eyes by Edmund de Waal

ARTICLES OF INTEREST

7 ARTICLES OF INTEREST:

1 Women On Boards Report: **https://www.gov.uk/ government/uploads/system/uploads/attachment_data/ file/31480/11-745-women-on-boards.pdf**

2 EU quota for 40pc of women on boards moves step closer **http://www.telegraph.co.uk/finance/newsbysector/ banksandfinance/10378585/EU-quota-for-40pc-of- women-on-boards-moves-step-closer.html**

3 Germany plans legal quotas for women on non-executive boards **https://www.gov.uk/government/uploads/system/ uploads/attachment_data/file/31480/11-745-women-on- boards.pdf**

4 The Economist **http://www.economist.com/news/business/21590372- more-women-boards**

5 Independent: Have a long way to go: **http://www.independent.co.uk/news/business/news/the- glass-ceiling-women-on-boards-we-have-a-long-way- to-go-9210255.html**

6 Tyson Report **http://www.icaew.com/en/library/subject-gateways/ corporate-governance/codes-and-reports/tyson-report**

7 Higgs Report **http://www.ecgi.org/codes/documents/higgsreport.pdf**

WHAT'S YOUR NEXT MOVE?

SO NOW you have all that advice, you have all those tips, you know what the traits and characteristics are, and you know what to look out for, I'm sure you are wondering how do you move forward? Well, here are a few more tips to help you on your way.

7 THINGS TO THINK ABOUT
BEFORE APPLYING FOR A NON-EXECUTIVE DIRECTORSHIP POSITION:

Now you have your tools in your tool kit – it's time to stop thinking and start working towards that job you always wanted, and never knew how to get! Here are a few more things to know before you set out on that journey.

1   **What do you have to offer that will add or fit in around the already well-rounded boardroom table?** Have a clear idea of your skills, what you would contribute and when. Make sure it's not only clear to you but clearly communicated, when putting it out there, that you are available for hire. Start with voluntary and public sector boards before moving up to the more competitive private sector and FTSE boards.

2   **Be present at all times.** In other words, ensure that you are over delivering in your day time job. Head hunters should be looking for you rather than you spending time in your day job looking for them. If you are good at what you do in your full-time job, the word will get around and they will knock on your door.

3   **Which head hunters are best for you?** Some will seek you out, but are they right for you? After you have decided which route you will take to the top, find the right vehicle on which to get there. If you are not attracting the attention you want, make sure you seek the ones you do. Different head hunters specialise in different fields, whether it's banking and finance, law, technology, not for profit, charitable or public sector. There are generalists, but most specialise these days. Find the right specialist.

4   **Raise your profile.** Get networking, get people talking about you, become the go-to person in your industry. Public speaking, specialist workshops, find a coach, mentor or sponsor in the place or industry you want to be in. Run a blog on your specialist subject area, write articles and even newsletters. Make it easier for the head hunters or even the company to find you on the internet. Brush up on your social media skills, tweet regularly, join LinkedIn groups, and if you feel confident enough why not YouTube your CV and tell people about your skills and what you have to offer. These things are easily achievable in this digital age. Ensure you do it safely.

5   **Brush up on your numeracy, P&L, and other financial disciplines.** No matter what discipline you bring to the table, one that will be called upon at every board meeting, and sometimes outside of the board, will be finance. If you don't have it you will be left behind on the most important matters. You need some understanding of company accounts and what they mean.

6   **Check them out because they will check you out.** Ensure that you know about any company that offers you a position. You will be responsible for what happens on that board, even if you know nothing about it. Know who you will be sitting

at the table with, and are they who you want on your side should things go wrong. Will you be in a position to defend them should it be the other way around. Feel comfortable and ensure you have a competent captain on that ship.

7 **Look before you leap.** It is tempting because you are eager to get started, but a little caution is advised. Ensure there is benefit to be gained for both you and the company you will join. When you feel ready and have taken advice, and only then, enjoy the ride

THINGS THAT MIGHT BE EXPECTED OF YOU ONCE YOU ARE ON THAT BOARD:-

* Uphold the highest ethical standards of integrity and probity.

* Support executives in their leadership of the business while monitoring their conduct.

* Question intelligently, debate constructively, challenge rigorously and decide dispassionately.

* Listen sensitively to the views of others inside and outside the board.

* Constructively challenge and help develop proposals on strategy.

* Scrutinise the performance of management in meeting agreed goals and objectives and monitor the reporting of performance.

* Be satisfied as to the integrity of financial information and that financial controls and systems of management are robust and defensible.

To find out more visit our website:

http://www.7traits.co.uk

WHAT'S YOUR NEXT MOVE NOTES PAGE

List 7 things you have learned and can **implement towards your next move:**

1 _____
_____
_____

2 _____
_____
_____

3 _____
_____
_____

4 _____
_____
_____

5 _____
_____
_____

6 _____
_____
_____

7 _____
_____
_____

COMPILE YOUR ROUTE MAP

NOW YOU'VE finished reading and making notes you should find this exercise quite revealing. Follow the last few steps to find your route map to the boardroom.

- ❖ After listing a minimum of three points that you would like to implement or would like to remember from each category of LEADERS, compile your list which should be around 22 points. Or you may wish to consider one point from each of our women on boards, and the things that NEDS have to consider.

- ❖ List on one page all the 22 tips, advice and ideas that you have collated through the book.

- ❖ Distil it down to a master list of 7 top ideas – one from each section, and see if it forms your personal route map to the top. Of course different people will get different answers and different routes, and the outcome is from a personal perspective formed from your responses.

- ❖ Enjoy the journey.

Disclaimer: This is not a scientific process, but an exercise compiled and tested by the author to give readers a route they could follow to the top. The outcome is dependent on the individual's responses.

ABOUT THE AUTHOR

Dr. Yvonne Thompson CBE has spent the last 30 years in the communications industry, most of which spent campaigning for minorities, small business owners and, closest to her heart, women's equality in the workplace, especially the boardroom. Having spent nearly half of that time being the only woman on a board with nine men, she experienced at first hand just how lonely being at the top can be for a woman. Having decided to share her experience, thoughts, hints, tips and advice to help other aspiring women, she also spent a year researching and talking to other highly effective women in boardrooms, and has chosen 22 of these top women's stories to share with readers.

This book is not about politics, is not about numbers, percentages and analytical research, but it will intrigue, inspire, and inform on what it takes to get to the boardroom, and what it takes to stay there. Stories, help, tips and advice from 22 women who made it to the top company boards, how they got there and how they stay there.

A dynamic, entrepreneurial business leader with a proven record for building high performing teams since starting her PR company over 30 years ago, Ms Thompson has acquired an exceptional range of transferable skills that can complement high-performing companies and organisations.

Originally from Guyana, South America, Ms Thompson has always shown an entrepreneurial flair. Not taking the usual channel to the small business arena, she evolved from freelance writing for many music industry newspapers including Music Week, the industry bible, and IPC weekly and monthly titles.

She has also been involved in many successful firsts in the UK including being Music Editor for the UK's first black monthly glossy magazine, 'Root', and also being a founder and director of the UK's first black music radio station, Choice FM, now owned by the Global Radio Group. Other firsts include starting the first black-owned PR company (according to PR Week), now known as ASAP Communications; running the first in-depth research of the lifestyle of the black community across the UK – The Black Consumer Survey, and starting the UK's first Black Women Business Network – The European Federation of Black Women Business Owners.

She also has over 20 years' experience on public sector boards for which she is well known. They include chairing the London Central Learning and Skills Council, DTI's Ethnic Minority Business Forum, African Caribbean Business Network, President of the first black women's business network across Europe, with chapters in France and Netherlands, The European Federation of Black Women Business Owners, the more recently founded, Women Business Leaders Network, along with many others where she brings energy, experience, dedication, and change to and for many.

Often called upon for media interviews on issues concerning small business, women and minorities, Ms Thompson is no stranger to engaging with Prime Ministers, Ministers, and high profile personalities in the business arena.

Having made her mark in the UK, she was awarded a CBE in the Queen's Birthday Honours List in 2003 for her services to women, small business and minorities. In 2005 she was awarded an honorary doctorate by London Metropolitan University for services to small business and mass communications. She has been recognized across the UK and Europe as well as internationally.

Ms Thompson has chaired many governmental committees, including the DTI (now BIS), the Learning & Skills Council and sat on various boards including the first Mayoral advisory board for the London Development Agency. Her most recent profiled roles include working with a prestigious corporate network, TNON (The Network Of Networks), and chairing the events committee for the Women's Diplomatic Service Network. Most recently, she was appointed to the Economics Honours Committee, where she is committed to help in their campaign to increase nominations from minorities and women.

Yvonne Thompson is committed to inspiring future leaders, and mentors future leaders through a leadership mentoring programme in conjunction with Deloitte and the Powerlist Foundation.

Yvonne works with a group of corporate BAME networks who produce Your Future Your Ambition, a careers advice exhibition aimed at young people age seven plus, encouraging them to take up STEM (Science, Technology, Engineering and Maths) as part of their educational enhancement and using role models within the corporate arena to show that jobs they thought unattainable can be theirs, given the right careers advice.

As well as speaking in schools and events to young people, she is also working with the Speakers for Schools campaign (Education for Employment), encouraging more women and minorities to go into schools to inspire young people on their career choices – again showing jobs they thought unattainable can also be achieved by taking the right path. She has particular focus on Inspiring Women (Speakers for Schools campaign) which is led by **Miriam González Durántez.**

She has run marathons to support and fundraise for Build Africa, a charity which has a school building programme across Kenya, Uganda and Democratic Republic of Congo.

Her most recent achievement since writing this book is that she was conferred by Plymouth University with another Honourary Doctorate of Business for Work in Enterprise, and the Global Diversity Agenda.

Find out more about the author:

http://msyvonnethompson.com

**7 Traits Leadership Learning Limited
2 Tunstall Road, London SW9 8DA**

Tel: **+44 (0)20 3086 9311**

Email: **7traits@7traits.co.uk**

Twitter: **@7traits**

LinkedIn Group: **7Traits**

Facebook Page: **7Traits**

Instagram: **7Traits**

Amazon: **http://www.bit.ly/seventraits**

As part of her ongoing campaign to promote more women into business, and especially onto boards, Dr. Yvonne Thompson CBE is an Ambassador for, supports and contributes to:-

BOARD APPRENTICE

BOARD APPRENTICE (BA) is a not-for-profit organisation dedicated to improving diversity and inclusion on company boards by widening the pool of board-ready talent.

BA believes that diversity goes beyond the visible diversifying aspects such as of gender or ethnicity to include those less visible aspects: age, social background, thinking style, experience, skill set and sexual orientation – among others.

There is a growing body of empirical research confirming the financial benefits of diversity yet, in spite of this, the current pipeline of potential directors is insufficiently diversified and closed off to many who are not in the 'right' pools, or not identified by gatekeepers, or lack board experience. New applicants for NED roles are often rebuffed: "You can't be on a board unless you are already on a board" and so the closed loop perpetuates itself.

BA is the brainchild of an independent NED, Charlotte Valeur. She recognised that boards need a practical way to address the problem of the undiversified pipeline and the concept of a seat for education at every board table is a beautifully simple, easily-implemented solution.

BA identifies and places high calibre, diversifying individuals as Board Apprentices on boards for one year to gain practical experience, through observation of their operation and dynamics. Apprentices emerge with the real-time experience necessary to qualify them to take on board roles and to mentor other apprentices.

To learn more about becoming a host board, a corporate member, an apprentice, or to set up Board Apprentice in your own country, please email to:

info@boardapprentice.com

www.boardapprentice.com

AS PART of her ongoing campaign to promote more young women to take STEM (Science, Technology, Engineering and Mathematics) subjects for going into the business arena, and especially onto boards, Dr. Yvonne Thompson CBE is an Ambassador for, supports and contributes to:

The national Inspiring Women campaign, launched in October 2013, already has over 16,000 women ready to talk with girls in state schools about the 'job they do' and the 'route they took'. Our ambition is to see these women from a wide range of occupations going into state schools and collectively talking to 250,000 young women in the next school year.

Our volunteers can be 18 year old apprentices or CEOs, work for themselves or for a multi-national, be working full-time, part-time or having a career break. Girls in state schools want to hear about their job, career and life experiences.

The national Inspiring Women campaign, which is part of the free, national Inspiring the Future scheme run by the Education and Employers charity, aims to increase the number of interactions between girls and women from all walks of life. Such interactions, for example through career speed networking events in schools halls, CV workshops, mock interviews and workplace visits, can help tackle gendered perceptions of careers and help young people develop self-confidence as well as useful contacts and networks.

Please sign up to volunteer here:

http://www.inspiringthefuture.org/inspiring-women/

Part of
Inspiring the Future

Inspiring
women

ABOUT THE AUTHOR

306

"YOUR FUTURE, YOUR AMBITION" (YFYA) is an ever expanding, inspiring annual event. This initiative works with a number of large organisations aimed at providing experiences and opportunities to school children and students in pursuing careers in Science, Technology, Engineering and Mathematics (STEM).

We bring together blue-chip organisations that embrace diversity and understand the value a diverse workforce brings to their business. These companies showcase their latest work in STEM through exciting activities and demonstrations for attendees to participate and engage in. There is also the opportunity for students to speak directly to company representatives about further education, apprenticeships and available career opportunities.

YFYA inspires, educates, informs, and motivates children and young adults into studying STEM based subjects. Since its launch in 2012, over 2,000 students have attended YFYA events, with 620 of them receiving mentoring.

YFYA caters to the following age groups:

- ❖ **7-11 year olds** – Visit our exhibition space, and sign up for our breakout sessions to find out more about Science, Technology, Engineering and Mathematics subjects.

- ❖ **12-16 year olds** – Speak to our exhibitors about how STEM subjects might lead to a career, and sign up for our topical breakout sessions run by some of our participating organisations.

- ❖ **17+ year olds** – Find out more about careers with our exhibitors and visit our seminars on soft skills and careers run by some of our participating organisations.

For more information visit: **www.yourfutureyourambition.com**
Or email: **enquiries@yourfutureyourambition.com**

Your Future,
Your Ambition

THIS IS **<u>NOT</u>** THE END:

I STARTED with two quotes and I will close this chapter with the same two.

"It's not information, but how you use it that is powerful."

I hope that you have read with interest, eagerness and curiosity about all the women I interviewed, as you can take something from every one of them, and put it into action for yourself. I have absolutely no doubt it will be more, but if you take away just one gem and use it, your time will have been wisely invested. The only way it won't work for you is if you don't use it.

So use it wisely.

"If you gather the collective wisdom of people who 'have made it' in life, you start to see a trend."

Oprah Winfrey

Let's keep gathering and let's keep trending.

If you find this enjoyable and useful, please share the inspiration by doing a review on our Amazon page. Thank You

FIND OUT MORE:

FIND OUT more about 7 Traits Leadership Learning including:

7 Step Women on Boards Programme*

7 Step Career Development Programme*

7 Traits Workshops including:

- ❖ Media Training

- ❖ Public Speaking

- ❖ Networking and Beyond

Plus our list of highly recommended Headhunters in the UK

Visit: **http://www.7traits.co.uk**

Email: **7traits@7traits.co.uk**

7 Traits Leadership Learning Programmes* are working towards certification by GSM (Greenwich School Of Management) Plymouth University.

RESOURCES

1   There is a wealth of resources which have been compiled on our website, including videos, free eBooks and discounted materials for advice, tips and practical training for L.E.A.D.E.R.S. career development. To access these, simply register for membership on our site at **http://www.7traits.co.uk**

2   The "personal profiling" book which has been written in tandem with this book is available discounted or free download at **http://www.7traits.co.uk** for those of you who have signed up for membership.

3   Information on our range of training, coaching and workshops can be found on our **website, http://www.7traits.co.uk**

4   If you would like to discover how to increase your chances of advancing up the corporate ladder, visit our website at **http://www.7traits.co.uk**

5   To learn more about these women and the companies they work for, visit our website **http://www.7traits.co.uk**

6   Watch the video interviews of our mastermind interviews. **http://www.7traits.co.uk**

7   To add your voice to the conversation, send us your tips and advice to our forum, and get credited for it, on our website at **http://www.7traits.co.uk**

Bonus Tip: For a list of our Top 10 Head Hunters, email **7Traits@7trait.co.uk**